FAIR LIBERTY'S CALL

FAIR LIBERTY'S CALL

SHARON POLLOCK

Coach House Press
Toronto

Coach House Press
760 Bathurst St., 2nd floor
Toronto, Canada M5S 2R6

First Edition
Printed in Canada
1 3 5 7 9 8 6 4 2

Published with the assistance of the Canada Council, the Ontario Arts
Council, the Department of Canadian Heritage and the Ontario
Publishing Centre.

Canadian Cataloguing in Publication Data

Pollock, Sharon
Fair liberty's call

A play.
ISBN 0-88910-488-3
1. United Empire Loyalists—Drama. 2. United States—History—
Revolution, 1775-1783—Drama. 3. Waxhaws (S.C.), Battle of, 1780—
Drama. 4. Yorktown (Va.)—Siege, 1781—Drama. 5. New
Brunswick—History—1784-1867—Drama. I. Title.

PS8581.O55F3 1995   C812'.54   C95-930770-2
PR9199.3.P65F3 1995

CONTENTS

DIRECTOR'S INTRODUCTION

Fair Liberty's Call may, at first glance, look like a traditional history play set amidst the Loyalist immigration to Canada after the American Revolution. Sharon Pollock, however, is less interested in a sequence of dates and events than in using history as poetry to explore the complex warp and woof of choice and responsibility in our country past and present.

Just as the early immigrants to this land had to clear and plough the soil in preparation for the planting of a life-sustaining crop, so each of Pollock's eight characters must metaphorically dig inward to clear the stumps and rocks and plough his/her own soul to prepare for an existence in a new home.

How culpable was George, the father, in the death of his two sons? And in the transformation of Emily into Eddie? Were his opportunist attempts to ensure the family's survival genuine but misguided? To what extent are the loss of property and the physical deprivations that the family has endured due to George's lack of principle, and to what extent are they "accidents of war"?

Should Annie be held responsible for the death of John Andre, the British spy who was captured trying to smuggle the plans of West Point through Rebel lines? Or was the manipulation of a human trust, gained through physical intimacy, excusable in wartime because it was done out of loyalty to Annie's Rebel brother Richard?

Did Eddie, who was once Emily, pick up the rifle of her twin brother Edward after he committed suicide because her father insisted, or did she do it of her own volition? If she now uses this same rifle to fight the Loyalist élite in its attempts to assume an oligarchical stranglehold on political power in the new province, will this absolve her of participation in the atrocities of war?

Daniel, Wullie and Major Williams are each forced at gunpoint to re-examine their actions at the battle at Waxhaws where defenceless Rebels were slaughtered as they attempted to surrender. Each character painfully revisits the choices he made on that day and must then accept his guilt in the atrocity. The honesty and completeness with which each character is prepared to dig into his/her own responsibilities will ultimately have a major influence on the nature of the new country that is in the process of being born.

John Anderson's presence, like a revenging angel, has the uncanny ability to conjure up in each of the other characters a memory of the dead Richard, or Edward, or John André. Ironically it is Anderson, the outsider, the Rebel, the American, who forces each of the Loyalist immigrants to embark on his or her journey of introspection and self-confession that will make a beginning in this new country possible. Yet even John Anderson, having arrived on the scene in search of justice, will return south of the border having laid his grief for his dead brother to rest. The new country, Canada, has an influence on the one south of the border.

As each of the other characters completes his or her internal journey, this permits Joan, the mother (whose suffering has distorted her mind to the point where she can see and hear realities beyond the ability of all others) to begin to appreciate the potential of her new home. At her arrival, Joan says of this country, "Your feet leave no trace of your passing." After she and each of the other characters have come to terms with their actions and responsibility and grief, she observes that now her passing over the ground actually leaves "a soft indentation in the dirt." The new immigrants are ready to leave their mark.

Meanwhile, in the woods surrounding the clearing where the reunion is taking place, the spirits of a previous civilization, one that lived in closer harmony to the earth itself, watch the actions of these invaders with a mixture of benevolence, curiosity and fear.

Not only is this the rare work of art which tries to understand present-day English Canada by exploring the past, but Pollock has dared to examine our identity in relation to our powerful neighbour to the south without resorting to cheap stereotypes. Rather, she is forcing *us* to come to terms with ourselves. "Where do you put your eye to find the heartbeat of a country comin' into being?" Sharon Pollock asks at the beginning of her play. One answer. "On ourself." We are all responsible for our own choices.

"Choice"—that most English Canadian of words, because Canada, with geographical, linguistic and racial forces threatening our integrity, is the only country in the world that exists solely by virtue of a choice that must be continually renewed by its citizens. What a post-modern idea of a country that is! Sharon Pollock has, with her extraordinary play, forced us to confront our own nationhood.

—*Guy Sprung*

BATTLES AND SKIRMISHES OF FAIR LIBERTY'S CALL

BUNKER HILL—June 17, 1775. The British, attempting to break the siege of Boston, successfully led 2,250 troops against about 2,200 Americans. In gaining an outpost of little value, the British suffered prohibitive casualties, 271 dead and 783 wounded to only 140 Americans killed and 271 wounded.

QUEBEC—December 30, 1775. A force of about 1,000 Americans under Gen. Richard Montgomery and Benedict Arnold were repulsed by 1,200 British under Guy Carleton. Over half of the American force was killed, wounded or captured, and the project to conquer Canada was abandoned.

SARATOGA—October 7, 1777. Moving down the Hudson Valley towards Albany, the British were confronted by more than 7,000 troops under Gen. Horatio Gates. Near Saratoga Springs, the American victory ended British plans to reduce New England and brought France into the war as an ally of the United States.

CHERRY VALLEY—On a foggy November morning in 1778, 200 Loyalist Rangers and 500 Indians burned, plundered and scalped the tiny village of Cherry Valley, 50 miles west of Albany, New York. This was one in a series of atrocities each side perpetrated on the other in an escalating sequence of retaliations.

CHARLESTON—April 1 to May 12, 1780 (seige). Unable to escape, the Americans held out for six weeks before the entire force surrendered. American casualties during the seige numbered 238; 76 British were killed and 189 wounded. The American army in the South was lost. The British proceeded to occupy South Carolina.

WAXHAWS—May 29, 1780, Waxhaws, South Carolina. Tarleton's troops advanced with the horrid yells of infuriated demons. When the Americans perceived further resistance was hopeless, they raised a white flag. Tarleton's men proceeded to slaughter the defenceless Rebels. It was the concurrent testimony of the few survivors that for fifteen minutes after every man was prostrate, the Loyalists went over the ground, plunging their bayonets into everyone that exhibited any signs of life. Tarleton's loss was 5 killed, 14 wounded.

CAMDEN—August 16, 1780, fought near Camden, South Carolina. The American militia fled and was routed, suffering at least 750 killed or captured to the British's 68 killed and 245 wounded. The disasterous defeat exposed North Carolina to easy invasion by the British.

KING'S MOUNTAIN—October 7, 1780, fought in South Carolina. A body of 900 militia from the North Carolina and Virginia back woods pursued and cornered a party of about 1,100 Loyalists. Fighting from tree to tree, the Patriots cut the British forces to pieces, killing 225, wounding 163, and taking more than 700 prisoners. The Americans lost only 28 killed and 63 wounded.

COWPENS—January 17, 1781, fought in South Carolina, at "Hannah's Cowpens" near the Broad River. Tarleton's troops were lured into devastating fire from the Continentals, and routed.

COWAN FORD—January 31, 1781. The British crossed the ford while the American guards slept. The bulk of American forces hurried to the scene of the action but by the time of their arrival, the Red Coats had scrambled up the bank, loaded their muskets and opened fire. The American militia fled in disarray.

YORKTOWN—September 28 to October 19, 1781, at Yorktown, Virginia. The decisive confrontation of British and Franco-American forces. Lord Cornwallis was entrenched there with 7,000 troops. By September 28, Washington had covered Yorktown on the land side with 17,000 French and American troops. All hope of escape gone, Cornwallis and the British troops surrendered on October 19, thus virtually ending the Revolutionary War. Allied casualties during the siege of Yorktown amounted to 72 killed and 180 wounded; British casualties amounted to 156 killed and 326 wounded.

FAIR LIBERTY'S CALL

Fair Liberty's Call was first produced by the Stratford Festival in the Tom Patterson Theatre, July 10–August 28, 1993, with the following cast:

JOAN ROBERTS: Janet Wright
ANNIE ROBERTS: Kristina Nicoll
EDDIE ROBERTS: Philippa Domville
GEORGE ROBERTS: Michael Hogan
MAJOR ABIJAH WILLIAMS: David Ferry
DANIEL WILSON: Ted Dykstra
MAJOR JOHN ANDERSON: Wayne Best
WULLIE: Tyrone Benskin

Director: Guy Sprung
Costume Designer: Maryse Bienvenu
Music composed by: R. Bill Gagnon & Geneviève Maufette
Lighting Designer: Kevin Fraser
Sound Designer: Evan Turner
Choreographer: John Broome
Fight Director: John Stead
Stage Manager: Janet Sellery
Assistant Stage Managers: Bruno Gonsalves, Theresa Malek
Production Stage Manager: Catherine Russell
Assistant Director: Paulina B. Abarca
Assistant Lighting Designer: Bonnie Beecher
Fight Captain: Wayne Best

Persons

JOAN ROBERTS, late 50's
ANNIE ROBERTS, Joan's daughter, in her mid-20's
EDDIE ROBERTS, Joan's second daughter, in her early 20's, who
has dressed and lived as a man since she was 16. She is an
ex-captain in Tarleton's British Legion, a Loyalist unit in the
American Revolution
GEORGE ROBERTS, husband of Joan and father of Annie &
Eddie, mid-60's
MAJOR ABIJAH WILLIAMS, mid-40's, formerly a major in
Tarleton's Legion
DANIEL WILSON, mid-20's, ex-corporal in the Legion
MAJOR JOHN ANDERSON, early 30's
BLACK WULLIE, early 30's, former scout with the Legion

Place
New Brunswick.
Time
1785.

In the opening segment, characters speak to the audience as well as
to each other. They have a compelling need to tell; to tell before
someone else tells; to correct a former mistelling; to tell before
they're unable to tell, or prevented from telling. This doesn't necessarily mean they are rushed, although they may be intense. They
are aware of each other; they may agree or disagree; they may har-
bour good or ill feelings, feel defensive or proud regarding past
actions or inactions—their own or others'—as revealed in the
telling. They may find some amusement in their past and present.

ACT ONE

A bare stage, the floor of which radiates in a dark-hued swirl of colour, represents the "virgin" land. Although this space appears empty and uncorrupted, it projects an aura of foreboding, a sense of the unseen. A subtle sound fills the space as if the air itself is vibrating just below the level of conscious hearing. There are several lightning-like flashes, each followed by a split second of blackness. JOAN *and* ANNIE, *each carrying a large bundle of belongings, and* EDDIE, *carrying a long gun, appear at the edge of the stage. They are followed by* GEORGE, DANIEL, *the* MAJOR *and* WULLIE. DANIEL *pulls a wagon, piled high with barrels, trunks and rough pieces of wood.* GEORGE *has a trunk lashed to his back, and carries a keg. The* MAJOR, DANIEL *and* WULLIE *carry long guns.* JOAN, ANNIE *and* EDDIE *step further into the space*

Following the lightning comes the sound of a rolling rumble of thunder, or of what might be thunder, for all sound is impressionistic, even surrealistic, rather than realistic

As the first three characters speak, the swirl of dark colours on the stage floor is gradually supplanted by dappled light evoking a glade in a stand of hardwood trees with sunlight filtering through the leaves. They speak over a taped montage of their own voices repeating the following words with some resonance

JOAN *You want to know where*
ANNIE *where*
JOAN *where to put your eye*
ANNIE *eye*
JOAN *eye so you can hear the*

ANNIE *heart*
JOAN *beat*
ANNIE *heartbeat*
JOAN *heartbeat*
ANNIE *of a country*
JOAN *country comin' into*
ANNIE *country*
JOAN *comin' into*
ANNIE *country comin' into*
EDDIE *country comin' into bein'*

> [JOAN, ANNIE *and* EDDIE *move further onto the stage and take their places at a distance from one another. Squatting on the back of her heels,* EDDIE *takes a crumpled piece of paper from her pocket and flattens it out carefully. It has blood on it. She wipes the blood on the front of her jacket, notices she has blood on her hand and rubs it into the fabric with her palm. Then she checks to assure herself that the blood is gone. She carefully folds the paper in eighths and places it in her pocket as* ANNIE *puts her bundle down and wipes her forehead*]

JOAN When first we come here after the revolution, when first we come … I saw a woman in the woods. A red woman. I saw her watchin'. Watchin' with a babe on her back. I saw her carryin' it like that, like—packed in moss, like—like nothin' I know. One mornin' I found a feather on the doorstep.

ANNIE We don't have a doorstep, Mama. We haven't had a doorstep since Boston. We may never have a doorstep again.

JOAN The feather was there. And in the sky a bird was circlin'. A bird like no bird I know. The colours were wrong, and the size. It circled three times. Three times. Then it soared up, up, wings outstretched, but not movin' its wings … This is a barren place. This wasn't home, isn't home, is no place I know, no, no place I know.

> [GEORGE *moves further into the space, places the trunk and keg on the stage and extracts a neatly folded British flag from his breast pocket.* EDDIE *assists him in guiding a white birchbark pole into place so the British flag may be attached and flown from this makeshift flagpole*]

GEORGE If you wanna know, I'll tell ya. Me, I'm George Roberts, formerly of Boston and one of that city's foremost citizens and merchants. And I never supported the Rebels! I lost every penny I had strugglin' against those traitors. I remained true to the King and to Parliament, and I lost everything, and I end up here with nothin'! To get somethin', I need to get in with the Committee of Fifty-five Families. Major Abijah Williams is the agent for the Fifty-five; Major Williams served with the Loyalist Legion; Major Williams fought with Eddie; and I think he's hot on my daughter Annie. Do you see where I'm goin' with this? Eh, Eddie?

[EDDIE *walks away from her father*]

Eddie!

JOAN Father [*indicating* GEORGE *with her right thumb*]. Mother [*indicating herself with her right forefinger*]. Four. Four Children [*extending four fingers of her left hand*]. Home [*her right hand folded into a fist*].

ANNIE We're here now, Mama. New Brunswick is home.

JOAN Four Children, Father, Mother, Richard, Annie, Em'ly, Edward, Home!

There was a table, a little table—there—in the parlour—and a sofa, there—and a whatnot in the parlour, yes! And a chair! Over there—and another one there! And it was all in a kind of maroon, a red, crimson red, a deep, dark red, and it was all— There was a rug! It was red! And a—

ANNIE He was nineteen, Richard, my older brother. Nineteen when he died. And Edward? My younger brother Edward? Killed himself at the farm in Tarrytown. That's a fact, we're dealin' in facts, aren't we? And Em'ly. My sister Em'ly?

WULLIE [*moving further into the space*] If you be a slave and owned by a Rebel, and if you run away and fight for the Loyalists, you'd be freed by the Loyalists. But if you did the same thing, and were owned by a Loyalist, you wouldn't be freed, no sir. Fightin' for the Loyalists won't buy you freedom 'less you be Rebel-owned and fight for the Loyalists.

Suppose you're a slave and you fight for the Loyalists. Before you could join the Loyalist exodus out of New York—after we lost the war—you had to prove you be previously Rebel-owned, and no runaway Loyalist slave. And once you proved that, you got what they call your certificate which says you're a free Coloured and can join the exodus, and you're eligible for land, 'cause you proved you weren't no runaway Loyalist slave.

EDDIE Wullie fought as a scout with Tarleton's Loyalist Legion. Wullie saved my life, but Wullie couldn't prove he was a Rebel-owned slave, could have been owned by a Loyalist ... so ... what're you going to do?... Proof be hard to come by. And without proof Wullie can't get no certificate. Wullie needs a certificate.

[DANIEL *pulls the wagon further into the space. With* EDDIE *and the* MAJOR, *he will alter and further delineate the space of the stage, taking from the wagon additional items to sit or stand on*]

DANIEL Whipped! I don't mind sayin' it. We got our Loyalist ass whipped by the Rebel Delaware Continentals. I thought we'd killed or taken 'em all at the battle of Camden but there they were, those Rebel boys turnin' up again as we come 'round the cowpens and Benny Tarleton, as he swings onto his horse, he says, he says "Kill every Rebel prisoner!" [*laughs*] Hell, we didn't take no prisoners! We were damn lucky we weren't taken *as* prisoners, eh Major?

MAJOR Do you remember Colonel Tarleton leadin' the charge, Daniel? His reins in his left hand, his right arm in a sling and no way to draw either gun or his sabre!

DANIEL I'd have followed him into the gates of Hell. Eh, Eddie?

EDDIE We did.

DANIEL You know, to think on it now, seems like kind of a foolish thing for him to have done.

MAJOR Courageous! Not foolish, courageous!

DANIEL He could have been killed.

MAJOR That's what makes it courageous.

DANIEL I wonder what he was thinkin' of doin' when he got into the thick of things, and him with only one useful hand and that hand on the reins.

MAJOR Do what he did do—charge with no means of defendin' himself! Lead his own men into battle with a cry on his lips. "Come
on my boys! Huzzaaaa!"

DANIEL "Huzzzaaaa!" he says!

MAJOR "Ride like Hell!"

DANIEL "And shoot like devils!"

EDDIE "And take no prisoners."

[*The sound of a whistle is heard, two notes rising and falling, bird-
like, followed by a dry rattle. The characters are aware of the sound.*
EDDIE, DANIEL *and the* MAJOR *share a flask, then rest a while from
their labours*]

JOAN That is not Edward. [*indicating* EDDIE] Edward is dead.

ANNIE That's right, Mama; he's dead.

JOAN Edward and Em'ly, both of them gone. Only seven minutes
between them. Yes, my belly was big, and the two of them,
they'd kick and tussle in there, and I'd sit, put my hands on my
belly like this, and I'd feel them, kickin' in there. I'd sit in the
parlour, ooohhh it was a wonderful room, it was all ... and ...
and, Edward came home ...

GEORGE Stop her.

JOAN then where were we livin'? not livin' in Boston

ANNIE How am I supposed to do that?

JOAN burnt outa Boston

GEORGE It's past, it's gone, Mama!

JOAN and not here yet

ANNIE Let her go. Get it over with.

JOAN Tarrytown! Livin' at the farm in Tarrytown! And Edward came
home from—from where did he come from?

ANNIE Cherry Valley.

JOAN And the Loyalist Rangers and he lay on the bed and his eyes,
what were his eyes?

ANNIE They were open.

JOAN And the pistol was where?

ANNIE On the table beside the bed.

JOAN And he wasn't the same. Sixteen he was—and—"He can't go back," I said to his father.

GEORGE Edward would do what was right.

JOAN Edward would do what his father wanted, that's what Edward would do, what he always did.

GEORGE Do what he wanted.

JOAN I was out in the hall when I heard it and as soon as I heard it I knew. I'd known since the day he came home. All that time I'd been waitin' to hear it. First the noise, and after the noise, the sound of the gun as it fell to the floor. A small kind of noise, not like the other, and then ... no noise at all. I stood there ... holdin' my breath, not breathin' ... and knowin' ... we ...

ANNIE Buried him.

JOAN We buried Edward and we said—

ANNIE It was Em'ly. We said it was my sister Em'ly.

JOAN Isn't that what we said? We said it was Em'ly. Dead. Of the smallpox. That's what we said. And Em'ly? She picked up Edward's gun—

GEORGE She wanted to do it!

JOAN —put on Edward's jacket, cut off her hair, joined the Legion, Tarleton's Loyalist Legion, Bloody Banastre Tarleton's Bloody Loyalist Legion! Because! Her father said!

GEORGE Because it was necessary!

JOAN It was Necessary! Because of Richard! Their Rebel Brother, our Son! Because of their Loyalist father! Because of you! Because of King and country and taxes and tea and—!

GEORGE It does no good. Hush, Mama!

JOAN And Annie was there when you drove Richard out.

ANNIE I was there in the hallway.

GEORGE Annie, please.

JOAN And Em'ly and Edward at the top of the stairs and all of them watchin' their own father drive their own brother out, drive Richard out! And he went!

ANNIE But he stopped.

JOAN At the end of the walk. And he turned. Even then, I don't think he'd have gone, but his father, he slammed the door. I ran to the window. Richard saw me—saw me there at the window—and he just lifted his hand in a bit of a wave—then he turned—and he went. My son Richard, who signed with the Rebels. My son! Son of liberty! Country, King, taxes and tea and round and round the Liberty Tree! Patriot Son!

ANNIE They're called Rebels, Mama.

JOAN But the English, they caught him, caught Richard. They had him with the Patriot prisoners packed and freezin' and starvin' in the holds of the English ships. Winter, and them in the holds below the water line in the East River! I begged! Good Loyalist man like your father? "Go to New York! Get leniency for Richard!" He could have done it, I begged! He wouldn't. I begged, and he wouldn't.

ANNIE Here are the facts—Papa was for representation in the English Parliament; Richard for separation and independence. And they fought, first each other, and then … It's true he was taken, held in the Long Island Prison Ships, and then—there was a prisoner exchange and later he died, we were told, in one of the battles they called Saratoga where he fought under Arnold. [*smiles*] That's right. Benedict Arnold. That's not fiction, that's fact. [*laughs*] He served under Arnold. Second time 'cause he served under Arnold at the Seige of Quebec. My Rebel brother served under Benedict Arnold. Isn't that funny?

JOAN That's when he sent Edward—him—[*indicating* GEORGE] her father sent Edward, he was only fifteen but he made him sign up!

GEORGE Edward wanted to go!

JOAN Edward signed with the Loyalist Rangers, went scalpin' and killin' all through the Valley, red Cherry Valley! His father thought that was going to balance things out! Richard there, Richard there, one Rebel son, and then poor Edward, the Loyalist. And when Edward died, make Em'ly go! Turn her into Edward, turn her into Eddie, Eddie take Richard take Edward take Emily. Three! Three of them gone! Murderer! [*to* EDDIE] You're a murderer!

[DANIEL, EDDIE *and the* MAJOR *resume transforming the space*]

MAJOR Cowan Ford!

DANIEL Cowan Ford!

MAJOR Cowan Ford as we was crossin' to the far bank!

DANIEL And the Rebels was firin' on us hot and heavy!

MAJOR Horses snortin' and us all hollerin' and drownin' and dyin'!
[*laughs*] You remember that, Eddie?

DANIEL I'm going to tell you somethin'. At Cowan Ford I seen Frank
Taylor—I seen him—there was this here Rebel boy firin' at us
and he fell into the water from off of the bank they was firin'
from—and the current got him. And Frank knew him, he knew
him, he recognized him like. And Frank he hollers, "Billy boy!"
he says. "Billy boy, it's me!" And he holds out his hand like so.
The Rebel boy, he looks up from the water, and he finds his
footin', and he starts splashin' and wadin' towards us reachin' out
towards Frank. He reaches out for Frank's hand. And Frank, he
ups with his gun and he fires.

MAJOR I never seen that.

EDDIE I seen it.

DANIEL And the Rebel boy he fell back, and the river took him. Took
him and the horses and our red-coated dead. The river took 'em
all. They floated away. [*pause*] Ah, what the hell. We're here. It's
a bloody miracle, but we're here. We may've lost everything, but
we are here. Yaaaaa-Hoo!

MAJOR Huzzaa!

MAJOR AND DANIEL [*singing, alternating words and phrases as they
prepare to leave the stage area*]

If ... buttercups buzzed after the bee
If boats ... were on land, churches on sea

[*The sound of a murmuring wind is heard, a dry crackle under
the song*]

If ... ponies rode men and grass ate the cow
If summer were spring and the other way 'round
Then ... all of the world ... would be upside down!

[*Voices call out to each other randomly: on top of each other, far off,
remote, echoing, faint, resonating. "Huzzaa!" "Come on my boys!"*]

"Remember the Cowpens!" "Ride like Hell!" "Shoot like devils!"
"Billy boy, this way, Billy boy!" WULLIE *follows* DANIEL *off. The*
MAJOR *stops and remains on the periphery in the shadows.* EDDIE
watches them leave. They seem to disappear into a smudge of smoke
that drifts from the upstage periphery of the space. The voices resonate
and fade as JOAN *speaks*]

JOAN Up in the woods where I saw the red woman, there are bones.
Leg bones of a man, maybe a man ... Arm bones. Part of a rib
Cage, and a Skull missin' the Jaw. Disarranged. When you stand
there, you feel your feet restin' on top of the soil. You could slip.
You could fall. Empty eyesockets catch your eye tellin' you some-
thin'. Your feet carry you back to the house but they leave no
trace of your passing ... This isn't home. They aren't our Dead.
The red woman stands in the glade of trees, and she watches.

[*A faint bird call followed by a dry rattle can be heard at random*
intervals as EDDIE *speaks*]

EDDIE If you be a Loyalist, colonial born, and you fought for the
English, and you got taken by Rebels, you'd not be exchanged,
for the English accepted the Rebels' namin' of you as a traitor.
But if you fought for the English and you be English born, and
got taken by Rebels, you could be freed, English-born soldier for
Rebel soldier, in a one-for-one prisoner exchange. Colonial born
you could rot in a Rebel prison. What does that tell you?

I served as a soldier, Loyalist, colonial born, bloodied my
hands and my arms, waded in gore, in the name of a King who
would condone his enemies' namin' me traitor. What does that
tell you?

Now, after the revolution, the Loyalist soldier was promised
land, land and material goods to start fresh in this new place, our
reward for remainin' loyal to the King. Three years later, the
Loyalist soldier is still waitin' for that reward. Instead of it, we
get absentee landlords, with the best land given to those who
already have power and pride and position! The ordinary soldier,
like you or like me, gets a remote or barren plot—or no plot at

all! Or he must submit to be a tenant and farm for the absentee landlord! What does that tell you?

And now those same who abuse us, and I'll name them—the Committee of Fifty-five Families—have put up a slate of candidates for election to office in the Assembly! What does that tell you?

Here's news, friends. There's opposition to the Fifty-five, and that opposition is mounting a slate of alternate candidates! What does that tell you? Exercise freedom of choice, citizens, or be party to your own oppression. Signed. "A Soldier."

[EDDIE *squats, with her gun, a distance from* GEORGE, JOAN *and* ANNIE. *The sound of the dry rattle stops*]

GEORGE Today is October 22nd, 1785.

JOAN What day's today?

GEORGE Today is a day for rememberin'.

JOAN Is that today?

GEORGE Four years ago today is the day the world turned upside down.

JOAN Today?

GEORGE That was the day Yorktown fell.

JOAN That's not today.

GEORGE That was the day we lost the war!

JOAN Day we lost.

GEORGE So there's reunion tonight! And rememberin'! And Tarleton Legion merry-makin'! And business tonight!

[*End of opening segment, no break in dialogue or action*]

ANNIE Look, I've burnt my hand twice, and singed my eyebrows and the front of my hair tendin' the porker for this bloody reunion.

[*A faint thunder-like sound rumbles*]

Rain—and now the coals in the pit'll go out, and we can all have pink porker, won't that be nice.

JOAN [*sitting alone, at a distance from the other characters, engaged in repetitious slicing of bread, cheese and sausage*] Pink porker, pink, pink porker, pink porker.

ANNIE What's that?

[GEORGE *is opening the keg*]

GEORGE Rum. The Major's here, and he's provided the rum. Where's the Legion standard? Eddie should've had it up and planted before dark.

ANNIE Is it dark?

[*It isn't*]

GEORGE You have a way with you, girl. I hope you marry a man with restraint. He'll need it.

ANNIE Who should I marry?

[GEORGE *is searching for the Legion standard*]

GEORGE Abijah Williams.

[ANNIE *laughs*]

Humour an old man, it's not such a bad idea.

ANNIE It's a terrible idea. Don't ever have it.

GEORGE He's in thick with the Fifty-five, and they're the ones to be thick with if you want to thrive in this neck of the woods.

[MAJOR WILLIAMS' *attention is on* GEORGE *and* ANNIE]

ANNIE Amongst other voids and vacuums of character, he is totally lacking in restraint—and well you know it.

[GEORGE *finds the Legion standard*]

GEORGE Where's Eddie?

ANNIE Not here.

[*The sound of the wind is heard. The light flickers*]

There'll be nobody come in this weather.

GEORGE Them that can come will come, and Eddie should be here to greet them.

[GEORGE *erects the standard near the wagon*]

ANNIE When you're finished take a look at the porker! Build up the coals under the porker!

[GEORGE *exits*]

MAJOR [*approaching* ANNIE] Porker is it?

ANNIE That's right, Major. When Papa heard there were pigs at the neighbours, over he went and brought into play every bargainin' trick learnt in a lifetime of buyin' and sellin' the empire's tea.

MAJOR Roast pig.

[*He savours the words as he eyes* ANNIE; *he gets out his pipe.* ANNIE *will light it and draw him a rum during the following*]

ANNIE He was determined. I think he'd heard roast pig was your favourite.

MAJOR And not too easy to come by.

ANNIE He'd have sold his soul for it, though I believe that went in exchange for the tent our first winter here. Or on some other occasion of need. Or demand.

[ANNIE *gives* MAJOR *a rum*]

To kill the last of the chill from your ride.

MAJOR It was a bone-chilling ride. It may take a bit more than the rum.

[*He grabs* ANNIE. *She struggles to free herself.* JOAN *is still sitting alone, preparing food.* EDDIE *glances up from her gun and observes the struggle.* EDDIE *gets to her feet*]

JOAN Like a bullet-hole in his head, like a rope catchin' you under the chin, like a narrow ravine, a depression, a dip, like a Valley! Like saltwater runnin' out of the bay, like the tide rushin' in through the gorge!

[ANNIE *manages to hit the* MAJOR *back-handed across the face with her clenched fist, not a slap. The blow gives him pause. The sleeve of* ANNIE's *blouse is ripped, exposing her arm.* GEORGE *returns*]

GEORGE The ... the coals are banked, and the spit's turned.

ANNIE And isn't it a terrible job? It's a terrible dangerous job for a woman. I've been at it all day, and the smell of roast pig and cracklin' has so permeated my clothin' that the Major here has just fallen on me as if I were a chop. Isn't that right, Major?

[*He smiles and takes a drink of rum.* ANNIE *extends her arm to her father*]

Smell.

[*He ignores her. She draws her arm across her chest and rubs her arm where the* MAJOR *has bruised it in their struggle*]

GEORGE Get me a rum like a good girl, eh.

[*As* ANNIE *draws him a rum, her gaze meets* EDDIE's *gaze.* ANNIE *gives* GEORGE *his rum and withdraws a bit, observing the men as she assists* JOAN. EDDIE *watches* GEORGE *and the* MAJOR; *she listens to them*]

What've you heard from the Fifty-five?

MAJOR Be better if Eddie were here.

GEORGE Why Eddie?

MAJOR The greater part of the cash you'll see in a year is Eddie's half-pay captain's pension, and your largest allotment's his acreage for Loyalist Legion service. Don't that give him a say in the matter?

GEORGE We're talkin' land allotment to members of the Fifty-five, and that's got nothin' to do with military service or rank.

MAJOR You forget, George. You're not a member of the Fifty-five.

[As GEORGE *speaks, the* MAJOR *removes a newspaper, the* Gazette, *from his pocket*]

GEORGE But I support them, don't I, and I support their Assembly slate for election. All I ask is material recognition through land allotment of my former position and loss as a citizen loyal to the Crown. The only real money to be had in this country is land. You know it and I know it. Land is money and money's land.

MAJOR Have you read the *Gazette?*

GEORGE The *Gazette*, why do you ask?

MAJOR There's an interestin' letter in the *Gazette*.

[*He passes the paper to* GEORGE *to read*]

Read it.

[EDDIE *approaches the two men. The* MAJOR, *seeing* EDDIE, *raises his rum in a toast that* EDDIE *acknowledges with a nod, as* GEORGE *continues to read the* Gazette. EDDIE *draws a drink of rum*]

To Tarleton's Legion—How many of the boys do you think'll make it?

EDDIE Some. Fewer than last year.

MAJOR Have you read the *Gazette?*

[EDDIE *nods*]

Interestin' letter in the *Gazette*.

EDDIE You think so, eh.

MAJOR The man who delivered it to the paper, as well as the printer? They've both been charged.

EDDIE With what?

MAJOR Seditious and scandalous libel. You'll note the article carries no name, it's simply signed "A Soldier". Of course the author's identity is known.

EDDIE I wrote it.

MAJOR The matter'll be carried no further, as regards legal action 'gainst that individual, given certain assurances.

EDDIE We've been robbed of our rights.

[GEORGE *crumples up the paper and throws it down.* ANNIE *will retrieve it unobtrusively when she gets the chance, smooth it out, and read it*]

GEORGE That's enough, Eddie!

EDDIE The best lots in town and country are reserved for particular persons, those bein' the Committee of Fifty-five Families.

GEORGE Whose position and placement warrant it!

EDDIE My father and me have been cheated and robbed in the matter of land, buildin' materials and clothin' owin' to us for my Loyalist service.

GEORGE I'm seein' to that!

EDDIE Is that theft now to extend to freedom of speech?

GEORGE That's [*the Gazette*] incitement to rebellion, that's what it is. You'd have to be blind not to see it, and a fool to write it!

MAJOR Listen, Eddie, your land registration could be expedited and your allotment expanded, some indentured persons could be made available—

EDDIE Slaves you mean.

MAJOR Indentured persons made available—if you could make available any information you have regarding—

EDDIE Inform, you mean.

GEORGE Listen to him, Eddie.

EDDIE I acted alone.

MAJOR We know there's division in the populace as regards the election and the Fifty-five's slate for Assembly so any information you might come across regardin' alternate candidates and their strategy would be welcome, that's all I'm sayin'.

EDDIE Quick—who does he remind you of?

GEORGE It's an opportunity, Eddie.

EDDIE The Rebels' Safety Committee in Boston, isn't that it? That band of vigilantes and hoodlums. I remember when they demanded allegiance to the Rebel Congress you swore allegiance to both Rebel Congress and Royal Crown. At the same time you denied allegiance to both Royal Crown and Rebel Congress, and all so eloquently done it prevented you gettin' tarred. Of course they eventually sorted it out and burnt the house, but by then we were well on our way to Tarrytown. Still, better the house than your hide, eh? But—I almost forgot—Major Williams here has his own Rebel Committee of Safety experience. Unfortunately he was not so eloquent in bestridin' two worlds, and I understand you lost two toes to a tarrin', sir.

[JOHN ANDERSON, *with a long gun slung over his shoulder, with his hands in his pockets, enters the shadows on the periphery, along with* DANIEL. *We aren't aware of their initial appearance, they are already there when, or if, we notice them*]

MAJOR I was eloquent alright. The smell of bubblin' tar makes a man eloquent. What I lacked was a son in the Rebel army.

GEORGE I had no son with the Rebels! I cut that boy out of my heart, and if it takes a tarrin' to show the world that, then I'd welcome a tarrin'! I have Eddie, and Eddie is foolish and simple and easily led!

[*The* MAJOR *moves to replenish his rum.* GEORGE *follows him. Midway through* GEORGE's *speech,* ANDERSON *removes his hands from his pockets. He carries a recorder, and he begins to play* 'Revolutionary Tea']

Eddie may give the appearance of a man, he may wield the gun and the sabre like a man, but Eddie needs guidance. Eddie will do whatever's required. For God's sake let's not leave it there.

[DANIEL, *with his gun over his shoulder, begins to march to* ANDERSON's *harmonica.* DANIEL's *drunk, having fun, keeping time with his "HuzZa! HuzZa!" as he marches*]

DANIEL Huzza! Huzza!

JOAN Lah da dah! da da da da da da da da da dah!

DANIEL [stops] Corporal Daniel Wilson! At your service and ready for grog, sir!

MAJOR Corporal.

DANIEL That's the Major—[taking EDDIE's rum] And here's me, Captain! Thank you, Eddie. And there's the pure sweet angel I been tellin' you about, ain't she a dream? You're a dream, Annie. I'm going to kiss the hem of your dress 'cause you're a dream and an angel!

[He gets down to do so. ANNIE pushes him over with the toe of her boot]

ANNIE You're drunk, Daniel Wilson.

DANIEL Of course I'm drunk. How the hell's a man to keep the blood in his veins from freezin' in this new land if he don't mix it with a bit of grog? It's a life-savin' measure, sweet Annie. Now! I want you all to meet—this here friend of mine—this—What did you say your name was?

ANDERSON Anderson.

DANIEL Anderson! And I met him like this! I'm comin' along the road there and I see him just off to the side shelterin' under some trees, like.

ANDERSON That's right.

DANIEL No grog, you see, so the cold was just creepin' into his bones. God, but you're beautiful, girl. When you boarded the exodus ship, and Eddie says "This is my sister," my heart beat like it never beat in six years of war. I got a good lot, Annie, it runs to the river—

EDDIE Is it registered?

DANIEL That'll come, Eddie, stay out of this. It's the last winter I'll spend in a tent. Will you marry me, Annie?

[ANNIE laughs and shakes her head "no"]

She's beautiful, isn't she? And her father is beautiful too! A beautiful man.

JOAN [*sings to* ANDERSON] *Hi says the little mournin' dove.*

ANNIE Hush, Mama.

DANIEL And this is her mother.

JOAN [*sings*] *I'll tell you how to win his love.*

DANIEL Where was I?

ANDERSON I was told I'd find lodgin' if I kept to the road.

DANIEL Whoever told you that's crazier than a hoot owl.

ANDERSON So it seems.

DANIEL So I said to him, him, under the trees there, I said, "Are you a military man?" "Yes," says he. So I says, "There's a few of the boys from Tarleton's Legion gatherin' tonight, and if George Roberts don't make you welcome, and the boys don't open their arms to a fellow soldier, than I'm George Washington's cat. So what do you say, eh? ... Meow?

GEORGE Welcome, welcome, I'm afraid my mind was off on somethin' else. More rum, Annie.

ANDERSON Thank you, sir.

MAJOR Anderson, eh?

ANNIE Where did you serve?

ANDERSON The Rangers, ma'am.

MAJOR Rank?

ANDERSON Major.

MAJOR Ah.

JOAN [*to* ANDERSON] Edward?

GEORGE Hush.

DANIEL Eddie served with the Loyalist Rangers 'fore Tarleton's Legion. Right, Eddie?

ANDERSON [*to* EDDIE] Prior to my enlistment perhaps.

EDDIE Perhaps.

DANIEL Where's the bits and pieces?

GEORGE We was just gettin' to that.

DANIEL How the hell's a man to remember with no surroundin's?

[MAJOR WILLIAMS, GEORGE *and* DANIEL *begin to drag out the totems, souvenirs, and trophies of war from trucks, boxes and containers. They will decorate both the space and themselves as they prepare for the Remembrance Ritual.* EDDIE *observes more than she assists, lending a hand when needed. An American Rebel flag is draped over one of the wagon shafts. A large picture of Tarleton pulling on his boots, and one of King George, will be raised to oversee the proceedings. The regimental drum and sticks, their Tarleton green uniforms, an elaborately embroidered, but stained, waistcoat, a uniform jacket with lace epaulettes stiff with stains, an iron helment, a black leather cap with a white skull and the words "Or Glory" on it as well as various regimental flags and colours are all displayed]*

DANIEL Gotta fill the place up with things that speak of the past.

MAJOR Else how's a man to know who he is.

[JOAN *and* ANNIE *draw near* ANDERSON]

JOAN Edward served with the Rangers.

ANNIE Edward hadn't the stomach for scalpin' so he left the Rangers, eh Mama?

ANDERSON If it's scalp or be scalped, you can't blame a man for scalpin', ma'am.

ANNIE Was that the choice?

[ANDERSON *shifts focus from the women to the men]*

DANIEL Lookey here! Lookey lookey here!

[*He holds up a Tarleton green jacket and throws* EDDIE *a second green jacket; they're dirty and well worn]*

Legion green for the occasion, and rookie see [*holding up his foot]* the best pair of boots I ever owned. Get your green on, Eddie.

MAJOR You're still wearin' those boots?

DANIEL These boots got a history, Major. I took 'em off of a Rebel, but a fella I know says they're English boots these boots, so that Rebel stole 'em off an English corpse—and I stole 'em off of the Rebel's corpse—so what do you say, eh? Round and round, eh, Major?

MAJOR I wonder where the others've got to.

EDDIE Probably heard you were here, Major.

MAJOR Look, here's the Rebel banner Frank Taylor captured at the Waxhaws.

DANIEL Ohmigod! Gone right out of my head, ain't none of you heard? How the hell could I forget?

MAJOR Heard what?

DANIEL 'Bout Frank Taylor! Frank! Shot dead out of his saddle south of town this mornin'.

MAJOR Frank Taylor's dead?

DANIEL That's what I'm tellin' you, shot out of his saddle—

MAJOR What happened?

DANIEL Nobody knows. And only one thing sure, it was no stray shot from somebody huntin' off of the road. It was someone he met. Someone who rode right up to him, leavin' just enough space 'tween him and that someone for the barrel of a gun. Boom.

GEORGE Who'd want to kill Frank Taylor?

DANIEL Damn near everyone who knew him.

MAJOR He was as sweet a man as ever you'd meet.

DANIEL He was a miserable bastard, and that's not news to anyone here.

MAJOR The war changed him.

EDDIE He came by it natural.

DANIEL The war just shone a light on it.

MAJOR Poor Frank.

DANIEL Poor be damned. I seen him at Cowan Ford.

MAJOR There wasn't a man in the Legion could work a bayonet or a sabre like Frank.

EDDIE And I seen him at Waxhaws.

DANIEL We ain't talkin' 'bout that.

MAJOR It was a bloody one alright and Frank—

DANIEL I said I don't want to talk 'bout the battle at Waxhaws!

ANDERSON I can understand that.

DANIEL No, you can't. You wasn't there, but I know what you heard. Let me tell you somethin'. It was nothin' more than a little white hankie the Rebels tied to a sword. How the hell's a man to see that in the midst of a charge?

ANDERSON Were they yellin' for quarter?

DANIEL I was followin' Tarleton.

EDDIE They got Tarleton's quarter alright.

GEORGE What do you mean?

ANDERSON Cut down, despite their cries of surrender and absence of arms.

DANIEL We ain't here to talk about that!

MAJOR Benny Tarleton was a bold and brutal man. The times called for that, and I for one was proud to serve him. I'll brook no talk 'gainst Tarleton.

DANIEL I ain't listenin'!

EDDIE Well, what we sowed at Waxhaws, we reaped at King's Mountain, Daniel, so it ends up fair all around.

[DANIEL *begins a heel-toe caper dancing around the space while the others continue their talk; he bends and bows, singing to himself, to* ANNIE, *to a stick of wood, improvising a dance and song to his boots*]

DANIEL *Round and round and round and round look at my boots dah da da da da dah Da da dah Eh Annie boots fine pair of boots look at my boots Da da da da dah I love Annie and I love my boots dah da dah da da dah and they're great boots da da da da da dah round and round I'm celebratin' these boots and I'm closin' my ears and my ears are closed and I love my boots ...* [*and so on*]

ANDERSON There was none of the Legion at King's Mountain.

MAJOR Eddie volunteered, along with our scout, Black Wullie. You should have stuck with the Legion, Eddie.

EDDIE I admit it. I transferred after Waxhaws thinkin' to escape Bloody Tarleton and I end up at King's Mountain, ain't that a joke?

GEORGE What's the joke?

EDDIE Well, there we was, crowded into a little hollow at the top of a hill, surrounded by Rebels, and we was throwin' down our arms, with Wullie and me havin' a kind of sense we'd heard it before as we start yellin', "Quarter! Quarter!" And the Rebels, they yell back, "Tarleton's Quarter!"

DANIEL I ain't listenin'!

EDDIE And they kept on shootin'. So we take off our hats, and we sit

on our hands and we keep yellin', "Quarter! Quarter!" and the
Rebels keep shootin'. [*she finds the irony funny*] We got Tarleton's
Quarter alright. Mercy sought, none given.

[*With the low sound of the wind, the odd puff of smoke continues to
drift from the upstage periphery*]

GEORGE And?
EDDIE And what? And after a while they got tired of shootin' so they
   rounded up what was left of us and hanged six for good measure
   on the march to prison.
ANDERSON Yet here you are.
EDDIE Yeah, well, me and Black Wullie got away one night.
MAJOR And run straight back to the Legion.
EDDIE Crawled be closer to it, back through the swamps to the
   Legion, Black Wullie and me.

[*A faint, echoing moaning is heard.* GEORGE *is the only character
who hears it*]

MAJOR And happy enough to be there. For Christ's sake, Wilson!
   We're not talkin' about Waxhaws. We're talkin' 'bout King's
   Mountain now!
GEORGE Did you come with a horse?

[DANIEL *stops singing and dancing*]

DANIEL No, I walked all the way in these wonderful boots. Of course,
   I come with a horse!
GEORGE Did you stable your horse?
MAJOR Why do you ask?
GEORGE I just heard a cat out there.
MAJOR Bloody country.
GEORGE It's the smell of the pork.

[MAJOR WILLIAMS, DANIEL *and* GEORGE *are collecting their guns
and moving off. Smoke drifts past them*]

JOAN Pink porker.

[*The sound of a dry rattle returns*]

EDDIE So you served with the Loyalist Rangers?

[ANDERSON *nods "yes"*]

Cherry Valley?
I once knew a boy with the Rangers. After Cherry Valley he rode
away home and put a bullet right here. [*touches her temple*] Killed
himself.

[EDDIE *picks up her gun and leaves.* ANDERSON *starts to follow her*]

ANNIE Stay, why don't you? Rum, guns, old soldiers, a wanderin'
horse and a wild cat could be a deadly combination, Major.
ANDERSON If you want.
ANNIE You don't like the rum?
ANDERSON On occasion I do.
ANNIE And this is not that occasion?

[*An echoing of the sound of a shot is followed by an echoing second
shot*]

Odds are they'll shoot the roast pig, the horse or each other.
JOAN [*to* ANDERSON. *He holds an attraction for her*] Richard?

[*The sound of the wind blowing grows a little stronger.* ANNIE *gets
herself a rum*]

ANNIE I was just wonderin' ... What I wanted to ask was ... What's
your given name, Major?
ANDERSON John, ma'am.
ANNIE John.
ANDERSON Major John Anderson.
ANNIE John Anderson!

[*She laughs and claps her hands together in applause.* JOAN *joins in.*
The sound of the wind carries a hint of murmuring voices]

JOAN [*indicating one thumb, then the other; one finger, then the other*]
Major John Andre, who carried the plans for Benedict Arnold ...

ANNIE An exact correspondence in time and space is what, John
Anderson?

JOAN John Andre, who prior to his capture by Rebels, spent the night
under my roof in Tarrytown ...

ANNIE A notable occurrence of events apparently accidental is what,
John Anderson?

JOAN John Andre travellin' under the name of Anderson ...

ANNIE Is coincidental, John Anderson?

JOAN Anderson John John Anderson Anderson John Andre!
John Andre while actin' for Arnold who led my Rebel son
Richard ... Richard led into battle ...

ANNIE Hush, Mama.

JOAN Richard.

ANNIE The fact is, and what my mother is sayin', is your name's the
same as the British-born spy who acted for Arnold. That Major
John Andre, callin' himself John Anderson, met with Benedict
Arnold behind Rebel lines and afterwards stayed overnight at our
farm in Tarrytown.

ANDERSON Is that a fact.

ANNIE The fact is. We were not so much behind the Rebel line, as on
it, which had a disconcerting habit of movin' while we remained
stationary.

ANDERSON A difficult position.

ANNIE That Major Anderson Mama mentioned—left in the mornin',
took the road to the right 'stead of the left and was seized by the
Rebels.

ANDERSON Unfortunate.

ANNIE An accident of war. He was hanged.

ANDERSON Instead of the traitor.

ANNIE You mean Arnold?

ANDERSON Benedict Arnold.

ANNIE Benedict Arnold, the traitor? Surely that depends on your

angle of observation, Major. Benedict Arnold was a Loyalist. If
he was a traitor what then would you call the Rebels?

ANDERSON He fought with the Rebels, for the Rebels, led the Rebels
'til he betrayed the Rebels.

JOAN I want to see your face.

[*The faint echo of a shot is heard*]

ANNIE Personally I'm for the cat.

JOAN You aren't my son, Edward.

ANDERSON No, ma'am.

JOAN You knew my son Edward.

ANDERSON I don't recall meetin' him before this evenin', ma'am, Nor
he me, I believe.

JOAN Let me look at your face.

ANNIE I notice you've a powerful recollection of some things, and
none at all for others.

ANDERSON An accident of war.

ANNIE Were you shot in the head?

ANDERSON [*smiles*] No.

ANNIE Major Andre, the only Anderson we knew prior to you, con-
cealed the plans for the defense of West Point 'tween the sole of
his sock and the sole of his foot. Would you hide anything there?

ANDERSON No, ma'am.

ANNIE No. A fightin' man wouldn't. If detained by the Rebels, be you
farmer or spy, the first thing they'd steal would be your boots.

ANDERSON A practice not restricted to Rebels, ma'am.

JOAN Who did you serve with, tell me?

ANNIE Shush.

JOAN There's somethin' about your face.

ANNIE Pay her no mind. So the Rebels hauled off his boots, and what
do they see? Why, this bulgin' outgrowth of sock. So off with the
sock! I imagine they thought 'twas money. Poor Major Andre.
He was a very charmin' man. I think he took quite a likin' to
me, wouldn't you say, Mama?

JOAN [*referring to* ANDERSON] Likin' to him.

ANNIE So his misfortune was not in takin' the wrong road, for

whatever reason, but in his naïve choice of the plan's conceal-
ment. What would you say?

ANDERSON Well ma'am, I'd—

ANNIE So many ma'ams—you're a charmin' man, too.

ANDERSON I think of myself as a reasonable, rational man.

ANNIE So what do you say?

ANDERSON Till I'm sure I've all the facts, I hesitate to state an opin-
ion. Have I all the facts?

ANNIE Actually, Major Andre was a little too charming. Like trifle is a
little too sweet. I've never liked trifle. We haven't had trifle since
Boston so I suppose something advantageous came out of the
war. So there are your facts. So what do you say?

ANDERSON I think it would be best to say nothin' except to assure
you that I'm nowhere near as sweet as trifle and considerably less
charming than Andre.

ANNIE Then you may call me Annie.

ANDERSON Would your father approve of that?

ANNIE My father approves of hardly anything and puts up with
almost everything. Call me Annie, and I'll sing you a song.

ANDERSON Annie.

ANNIE Would you like the song you were playin' when you arrived?

ANDERSON What song was that?

[ANNIE *begins to sing and dance and is joined by* JOAN *who enjoys
dancing to the song*]

ANNIE AND JOAN *There was an old lady lived over the sea*
And she was an Island queen
Her daughter lived off in a new countrie
With an ocean of water between
The old lady's pockets were full of gold
But never contented was she
So she called on her daughter to pay a tax
Of three pence a pound on her tea, her tea
Of three pence a pound on her tea
The tea was conveyed to her daughter's door
All down by the ocean's side

And the bouncin' girl poured out every pound
In the dark and boilin' tide

[GEORGE *appears and hears the song*]

And then she called out to the Island Queen
Oh mother dear quoth she
Your tea you may have when 'tis steeped enough
But never a tax from me, from me
But never a tax—

[GEORGE *enters the space*]

GEORGE What the hell're you doin', what're you singin', girl? What
   the hell my apologies, Major, she's—
ANNIE Major Anderson doesn't mind, do you, Major?
ANDERSON You've a lovely voice.
MAJOR And it's not to be raised in a Rebel ditty!
ANNIE Didn't you sing that song?
GEORGE This girl has a way of wrappin' you 'round with words and
   then she tightens them up 'til your eyes pop out and you're
   strugglin' just to draw breath.
ANNIE Didn't you sing that song?
GEORGE Yes, I sang that song! I sang that song like many a good
   Loyalist! I sang and sang 'til I realized our troubles had nothin' to
   do with the principles of taxation and everything to do with a
   treacherous movement for separation and independence! There!
   Are you satisfied!

   [EDDIE *can be seen on the periphery. She lifts her gun and sights.*
   DANIEL, *unseen by* EDDIE, *approaches. He looks to see what she's*
   aiming at]

ANNIE So it's not necessarily a Rebel ditty. What would you say,
   Major Anderson?
ANDERSON I'd say it depends on your angle of observation, ma'am.

[*As* EDDIE *fires,* DANIEL *shoves the barrel of the gun up in the air. The sound of the shot resonates, echoes, then fades away. The* MAJOR *yells from off stage*]

MAJOR Hey!

DANIEL What the hell're you doin'?

GEORGE What's that?

DANIEL You were shootin' at the Major.

MAJOR Hey there!

DANIEL All clear, sir! All clear!

GEORGE What's goin' on?

DANIEL Jesus Christ, Eddie.

EDDIE What's wrong?

DANIEL You were about to part the Major's hair there and you're askin' me what's wrong?

[*The* MAJOR *enters*]

EDDIE I got on my old Legion green and my gun in my hand, and damned if I don't think I see me a traitor. So a crack of the gun and a nice bit of leaf just driftin' down on his head.

DANIEL You could have killed him.

EDDIE If I'd really been aimin' at the Major there, I'd've hit the Major, 'cause I've a fine eye with a gun. Ain't that right, sir?

[*The* MAJOR *slowly nods "yes"*]

GEORGE No harm done, that's the main thing, eh?

DANIEL If I hadn't—

GEORGE A joke, Mr. Wilson. No harm done.

DANIEL Well then—that's—some sense of humour there. [*laughs*] Going to rain, eh, going to rain greenery on you while you was just pullin' at a bit of that pig cracklin' and it's a wonderful firepit you got there, Mr. Roberts, and I'm going to build me one just like it, you move me to diggin', I'm inspired to dig—and to eat—and to drink—'cause I says them that ain't here ain't comin' here!!

[*More rum is poured; the bread, cheese and sausage is served by* ANNIE *and* JOAN. *Sometime during the following they light two lamps which they get from the wagon. They are silent observers of the men.* ANDERSON *is watchful, cautious*]

MAJOR McMillan never missed a Legion gatherin' yet.

DANIEL But he always come with Frank and there ain't no use waitin' for Frank, eh Eddie? Boom. Rode right up to him, somebody did—you know for a moment there, when I seen you under the trees, I thought of Frank.

ANDERSON Did you?

DANIEL Didn't you notice? So I just laid my gun 'cross the saddle, rested it there like that. Had it at hand, in case, you know.

ANDERSON I noticed.

DANIEL Do you think McMillan could have done that to Frank?

MAJOR Never.

EDDIE Frank was one of the Fifty-five.

DANIEL That's right.

GEORGE What's that got to do with killin' a man?

EDDIE Maybe nothin'. Maybe somethin'.

DANIEL Eddie's right. Frank was one of the Fifty-five and Frank got his full land allotment as promised while the rest of us is practically squattin', no registration, no nothin'.

EDDIE And the most part of Frank's land seized from a soldier's widow.

MAJOR Who had not registered the land properly.

EDDIE Say some.

DANIEL Well how come she couldn't register right and Frank could? That's the question.

EDDIE There's some find it easy and there's some find nothin' but blocks thrown in their way by the very ones supposed to be helpin'.

GEORGE That's enough.

DANIEL He's right.

MAJOR You know no more of the problem than a fish knows of flyin'.

EDDIE We know one thing! We know the agents directed to act in the interests of all are actin' on behalf of the Fifty-five and we know you're one of them!

MAJOR What the hell did we fight for if not the preservation of worth and class that's the very foundation of Empire?

ANDERSON [*to* EDDIE] What did you fight for?

GEORGE Eddie fought for King and Country knowin' the English parliament's treatment of us was an act of human frailty.

MAJOR That could be corrected in time by good men workin' within ordered and proper procedures.

GEORGE If worst come to worst preferrin' one tyrant three thousand miles away to three thousand tyrants one mile away.

MAJOR The rule of the mob.

EDDIE The people.

MAJOR You talk like a Rebel.

EDDIE I speak of the betrayin' of what we was promised and you call me Rebel? Me who's killed Rebels from Waxhaws to Camden, King's Mountain to Yorkton!

MAJOR What you speak is sedition and treason and best forgot by all of us here.

EDDIE Is any opposition rebellion?

GEORGE It's not the time for questionin'! It's a time for restorin' order and rank and stability. It's a time to get on with our lives.

EDDIE So our promised land, our great new province, this country will become the fiefdom of a few, is that it?

GEORGE Our position—

EDDIE Former position—

GEORGE —gives us rights, can't you see that?

EDDIE It's not what I'm lookin' at.

MAJOR Had your father been in New York when the Committee of Fifty-five Families was formed, why of course his name as a foremost citizen of Boston'd be there with the rest.

GEORGE You hear that, Eddie? So we benefit from the state of things. It's just a matter of declarin', publicly declarin' so to speak, for the Fifty-five.

EDDIE And for the election of their slate for Provincial Assembly.

GEORGE You see, Eddie listens.

MAJOR And that which I mentioned before, about the alternate candidates and their strategies, that information too should be forthcomin' from you, Eddie.

EDDIE And Daniel here, what's in it for him?

DANIEL I got no position but I sure as hell would like to get my plot registered.

EDDIE And if they decide to come and throw you off like the widow woman and give it to someone who stands higher with the Fifty-five, what then?

DANIEL Jesus, Eddie—I—I've trusted the Major here with my life on occasion, I guess I'd just have to trust him with my land registration.

GEORGE You see, Eddie?

EDDIE And what about them that aren't here tonight, what about their land registration?

DANIEL I dunno, Eddie! I got enough trouble lookin' after myself, what else do you want me to do?

GEORGE That sense of justice and fair play, that's a good thing, but it's got to be tempered with a sense of reality, Eddie. You'll learn.

EDDIE You don't know who I am or what I think.

GEORGE 'Course I do.

EDDIE You think you do but you don't.

GEORGE What kind of crazy talk is that?

EDDIE Let's talk about smashin' a man's skull with the butt of my gun, and wipin' his brains off of my sleeve. Or leanin' down from my horse and slicin' a man who's run out of powder, knowin' to stay my arm can mean my own death or the death of my friends. Let's talk about sightin' down the barrel of my gun and seein' the face of a neighbour, knowin' I might see the face of my brother sightin' down the barrel of his gun at me! And for what? That's what's crazy!

GEORGE No more, no more!

MAJOR There's some things have to be done and we had to do them.

EDDIE To stop and think then was to die, but now? Now I ask, what did we do it for?

MAJOR Loyalty to our country, trust in Parliament and the King.

EDDIE Are they to be trusted?

GEORGE Eddie—

EDDIE You know nothin' about it and you know nothin' 'bout me!

GEORGE I'm your father, I know you better than anyone! You sit down, sit down! The rum's gone to your head.

[*Several quick flashes of lightning are followed by a roll of thunder, which echoes and fades. A faint dry rattle is heard*]

DANIEL We're not here to argue and fight, we're here to remember. Where's your green, Major, the Legion jacket that took you to war? I'm wearin' mine, and Eddie's got his, where the hell's yours?

[*He tosses a green jacket to the* MAJOR]

There you go, Major.

MAJOR [*as he struggles into his green jacket*] The damn thing has shrunk.

DANIEL Or your belly has grown, eh Eddie? Come on Eddie! Ta-dum! Ta-dum! There you go, Major, this one should fit, ta-dum!

[*The* MAJOR *puts down the green jacket.* DANIEL *throws the iron helmet and the uniform jacket with the lace epaulettes to the* MAJOR. *He will wear both although they do not fit*]

Ta-dum! A toast! A toast! Rum all around! There may be just a few of us here, but we're still rememberin'—that's what we're here for. What else are we here for, Major?

[GEORGE *puts up a large picture of Tarleton*]

DANIEL [*a toast*] Here's to Tarleton's Legion!

MAJOR Here's to them that served and fell!

Here's to them who can't be with us!

DANIEL And may the Rebels burn in Hell!

[DANIEL *pounds on a drum and the others, with the exception of* ANDERSON, JOAN *and* ANNIE, *drink the toast. They are moving into the formal ritual of their Remembrance Ceremony, taking up positions, ready for speeches. The sense of occasion is undercut every once in a while by a comment or reaction not appropriate to the ceremony.* DANIEL *sings solemnly, as he would a hymn; it's the song that the Loyalists sang in defiance as they surrendered to the Rebels at Yorktown, the battle that marked Britain's defeat]*

If buttercups buzzed after the bee
If boats were on land

[*The* MAJOR *joins in*]

Churches on sea

[GEORGE *joins in*]

If ponies rode men and grass ate the cow
If cats should be chased into holes by the mice
And mamas sold babies for just half a crown
If spring were summer and the other way round
Then all of the world would be upside down!

EDDIE And not such a bad thing if it were.

GEORGE [*clears his throat; it's the first time he's participated in the remembering*] May I say somethin'? ... I want to say somethin'. I may not have had the honour of servin' with Tarleton, but I admire and envy you all. With two of my—With Eddie away, my job was to see to the women, my good woman and Annie. As to the rememberin', I can't share that with you, much as I'd like to, but joinin' you tonight, I'm going to take the liberty of donnin' my one and only trophy of war—and this, sirs, is it.

[GEORGE *holds up a blood-stained waistcoat*]

ANDERSON Where did you get it?

GEORGE [*as he struggles into it*] Well sir, when the Rebels fled Bunker Hill—gimme a hand, Abijah—with the English hot on their heels, a few loyal citizens like myself were there for what help we could give—I'll just leave it open—and we were checkin' the Rebel fallen—

EDDIE Were you?

GEORGE What?

EDDIE Checkin' the Rebel fallen?

GEORGE I just said I was.

EDDIE Were you lookin' for Richard?

GEORGE I was not lookin' for anyone! Listen to what I say! I say me
and a few others were checkin' the fallen and I come on this figure lyin' face down in the mud ... a young man, with a ruffled
shirt and a blue waistcoat and a blond head of hair. He'd been
leading the Rebel charge and he lay in the mud ... but his
hair—it still looked tidy and combed.

[ANDERSON *takes a drink of his rum.* GEORGE, *in the telling, feels a
sense of shame he hadn't felt at the time*]

And I ... I—took the man's waistcoat ... this is his waistcoat ...
the waistcoat of one of the Rebel fallen ... at Bunker Hill.

ANDERSON [*referring to what the* MAJOR *has donned*] And that is the
helmet of Baron de Kalb who led the Rebel forces at Camden—
and that is his jacket with the lace epaulettes that he wore at the
battle of Camden.

MAJOR Where almost two thousand Rebels flung down their muskets,
turned tail, and run! Huzzaaaa!

ANDERSON De Kalb and the Delaware Continentals didn't run.

MAJOR True enough.

ANDERSON Five hundred Rebels against two thousand Royalists! De
Kalb and the Continentals stood firm. But when Tarleton's
Legion charged, de Kalb went down. He was dyin' and one of
you hauled him up, propped him 'gainst a wagon, and twisted
him out of his coat! And he stood there, clingin' to the wagon
while the blood poured through his shirt and his breeches.
Which one of you boys was it?

DANIEL [*uneasy*]We're talkin' 'bout Yorktown.

EDDIE I don't recall the Loyalist Rangers bein' at Camden.

MAJOR I know goddamn well they weren't.

DANIEL To hell with Camden! Did you serve at Yorktown?

ANDERSON I was there.

DANIEL Well we're rememberin' Yorktown! Now! [*back to the
ceremony*] I can see that place on the inside of my eyeballs. I can

hear it in my ears. The band playin' sweet and pure, "If butter-cups buzzed after the bee ..." And then the silence. I can hear the quiet with us marchin' out to the surrender ground ...

MAJOR 'Tween two lines of Rebels

DANIEL I seen George Washington there on a big bay horse. You seen him too, Eddie.

EDDIE Who did you say you served with at Camden?

DANIEL I thought we was rememberin' the surrender at Yorktown!

MAJOR We are!

DANIEL Alright then!

[*He gives a roll on the drum*]

We was wearin' our Tarleton Loyalist Legion Green, and the Rebels, they had hardly no uniforms at all, they was wearin' old huntin' shirts, or a kind of brown shirt—

EDDIE [*low to* ANDERSON] What were you wearin'?

MAJOR The British in red, scarlet red—

DANIEL Was like wearin' a bullseye tied to your chest in the woods.

MAJOR They was never meant to fight in woods! Proper battle fields was what they were meant for!

DANIEL And—our Hessian allies? Four foot of hat, boots up to their arse, big bloody sword hangin' down catchin' in the bush every step they took, no wonder we lost the war!

MAJOR We're rememberin' Yorktown!

DANIEL I'm rememberin' Yorktown!

MAJOR Well you're not rememberin' right!

EDDIE For Christ's sake let's get on with it.

GEORGE *If buttercups—*

MAJOR The band playin'—

DANIEL *If buttercups buzzed after the bee—*

MAJOR Marchin' out, layin' down our arms, men weepin'—

DANIEL And little Charlie Meyers who busted his drum rather than give it over to Rebels—no Rebel drummer boy'd beat on his drum—and this here's the drum Charlie was give in New York, the only belongin' the boy had to transport when we sailed to this place—

MAJOR The beat of the drum, the scream of the fifes, and the—

DANIEL I want to remember Charlie Meyers.

MAJOR Charlie died after the war.

DANIEL I don't give a damn! This is his drum and I want to remember him, eh Eddie?

MAJOR Later, Corporal.

DANIEL Now, Major! I'm going to remember little Charlie Meyers who died in my arms of—What did he die of, Eddie?

ANNIE The cold and the crowdin' and the stinkin' smells of the exodus ship.

DANIEL ... who died ... in my arms. He was a good boy and would have been ... an asset! to this god forsaken place ... had he got here!

[*Pause*]

MAJOR Are you finished?

DANIEL I'm finished.

MAJOR And the clatter of grounded arms!

[*Pause*]

DANIEL Is that it?

MAJOR That's it.

[DANIEL *gives a roll of the drum, then tosses it to* EDDIE *who beats it as* DANIEL *grabs the* MAJOR, *singing and dancing with him*]

DANIEL *Come!*
  'Round the heather
  Come o'er the heather
  [*to* EDDIE] Play!
  You're welcome late and early
  Around—[*to* EDDIE] *are you playin'*?
  Around him fling your royal King

[DANIEL *"flings" the* MAJOR *at* GEORGE; *they dance together as*

[DANIEL *grabs* ANNIE. *The dance becomes faster and faster, more and more frantic, as all sing.* EDDIE *drums.* JOAN *does her own little dance*]

For who'll be King but Charlie
Charlie likes to kiss the girls
Charlie likes the brandy
Charlie likes to kiss the girls
Whenever they come handy

[DANIEL *kisses* ANNIE *who pulls free of him, laughing, as the song and dance continues.* MAJOR *collapses coughing and laughing.* GEORGE *grabs* JOAN *and the two of them dance.* WULLIE, *with his gun, enters, and is a shadowy figure on the periphery, watching, coming closer*]

GEORGE [*sings as* ANNIE *and* DANIEL *speak*]
Charlie likes to hold the girls
Charlie likes the brandy
Charlie likes to kiss the girls
Whenever they come handy ooooohh
Come 'round the heather

ANNIE You and your drum and your dancin', I never met a sillier man, Daniel Wilson.

DANIEL I fell in love with you the first time I seen you. Marry me, Annie!

[WULLIE *moves on with his gun.* GEORGE *is out of breath;* JOAN *slaps his back.* EDDIE *is the first to notice* WULLIE]

EDDIE Wullie?

WULLIE What be happenin' here?

DANIEL Legion get-together, Wullie!

MAJOR Anniversary of the Fall of Yorktown.

EDDIE You'd have had an invite if I knew you was 'round.

WULLIE Today be the 22nd.

MAJOR That's right.

WULLIE You be three days out.

EDDIE Annie, how about a rum for Wullie?

WULLIE Fall of Yorktown be October 19th.

MAJOR October 22nd

WULLIE No sir, 19th.

DANIEL [*laughs*] I think he's right.

MAJOR So what're you here for then if you think the rememberin'
should be the 19th and this here's the 22nd?

WULLIE Ole Frank be here?

DANIEL Frank's dead, Wullie.

WULLIE That true, Eddie?

EDDIE True enough. He took a ball through the chest south of town
this mornin'.

WULLIE Frank Taylor's dead?

DANIEL You look like hell, what've you been doin'?

MAJOR I said, if you ain't here for the gatherin', why're you here?

EDDIE Can't a man visit a friend?

MAJOR Wullie?

EDDIE He don't answer to you. How's Shelbourne, Wullie?

MAJOR Wullie!

EDDIE Keep your mouth shut 'til he's welcomed proper! This here's a
man who's closer to me than any man, and by God, Wullie, it's
good to see you.

WULLIE Frank's dead?

EDDIE That's right.

DANIEL Jesus, man, you're skinny, ain't they got no eats in
Shelbourne?

WULLIE Coloureds done be run out of Shelbourne, we over in
Birchtown now. People sold everything, now they starvin' and
sellin' themselves back into bondage.

EDDIE What about your land allotment and rations?

WULLIE Molasses and meal, and that give out after white rations.
Most often, nothin' left.

EDDIE And the land?

WULLIE We can't get title.

EDDIE Again the King's gratitude to Loyalists, eh Major?

WULLIE [*starting to laugh*] Frank Taylor's dead, right, Eddie? [*he puts
down his gun*] He's dead and here I be, walkin' on my feet,

crawlin' on my belly all the way from Birchtown to here, and you tell me Frank Taylor's dead? I come all this way to get you to read this and help me—

[*He takes a document from his pocket and shows it to* EDDIE]

—and Frank Taylor's dead!
MAJOR It don't call for laughin', boy.

[WULLIE *notices* ANDERSON, *but his attention is pulled back to* EDDIE]

DANIEL What's it say?
EDDIE It's an indenture agreement ... 'tween Wullie and Frank ... back into bondage—for thirty-nine years, Wullie?
WULLIE Ole Frank tole me one year, but it don't matter now, eh Eddie?
MAJOR Frank's got heirs, ain't he?
EDDIE What'd you sign this for?
WULLIE Ole Frank come to Birchtown and he tells me I ain't no freed slave.
EDDIE You got your certificate, did you show him that?
WULLIE Frank say he's going to swear he heard you and me Eddie, us talkin' 'bout I couldn't get no certificate 'cause I can't prove I run away from a Rebel. Frank say my certificate be false, be forged, got your writin' on it and be no good. He swears he heard us talkin' 'bout doin' that and he say he need a big black man like me. If I make my mark, one year service, he won't say nothin' ... We starvin' and freezin' in Birchtown, so I ... I make my mark.
MAJOR You're in trouble.
WULLIE After, I looks at the paper and I looks at the paper, and I gets to thinkin' 'bout Frank and I gets scared. Thirty-nine years you say? When he tells me one? Ain't that just like ole Frank?

[EDDIE *burns up the document in the flame of one of the lamps*]

MAJOR You think that's the end of it? He's property. He goes with the goods and the rest of the real estate.

[ANDERSON *will make a slow, subtle move towards his gun and pick it up*]

WULLIE But I has my certificate sayin' I'm free.
MAJOR You just told us Eddie got you that.
WULLIE The certificate's good, ain't it, Eddie?
EDDIE It's good.
DANIEL Well it don't make no difference, the Major says you be Frank's property now, burnt up indenture paper or not.
MAJOR Where was you this mornin'?
WULLIE Me, I be—
MAJOR Was you south of town?

[WULLIE *makes a move for his gun*]

Take him!

[DANIEL, MAJOR *and* GEORGE *seize* WULLIE, *who resists. They wrestle him to the floor with difficulty.* EDDIE *tries to assist* WULLIE. ANNIE *and* JOAN *watch. Just as* WULLIE *is subdued,* ANDERSON *fires a shot in the air from his long gun. He pulls the flag from the wagon shaft. The faint sound of the band playing "The Day the World Turned Upside Down" fades in.* ANDERSON *stands with the flag draped over one arm, his gun covering the others. The light falls as the music rises*]

ANDERSON Gentlemen!

[*The men and women look to him as he stands with the gun aimed at them. The sound of the band increases*]

[*Blackout*]

ACT TWO

"The Day the World Turned Upside Down" is fading as light comes up on the scene as seen at the end of Act One

ANDERSON Gentlemen.
DANIEL You could have just given a whoop.
MAJOR No need for weaponry, friend.
GEORGE No sir, he's collared.

[ANDERSON *makes a motion with the gun, and they drag* WULLIE *to his feet and shove him in that direction.* ANDERSON *motions for them all to move in that direction*]

ANDERSON All of you.
DANIEL Eh?
ANDERSON All of you.

[*They move together*]

The knife.

[WULLIE *tosses his knife to* ANDERSON]

MAJOR It's the black killed Frank.
GEORGE Don't worry, it'll all be legal and proper.
MAJOR We gotta take him into town and hang him.
DANIEL I'm thinkin'—

[ANDERSON *draws a pistol from his jacket*]

GEORGE We can't allow you to take him. He's gotta go into town.
    He'll get justice on Friday.
DANIEL Who t'hell are you anyways?
WULLIE I know the man's face.
DANIEL Who is he?
WULLIE I be scoutin' behind the line and I gets picked up by Rebels
    and this one be one of them Rebels.
ANDERSON And you played the Patriot Buck and we let you go.
WULLIE He be with de Kalb and the Continentals then.
ANDERSON Washington's Delaware Continentals.
GEORGE A goddamn Rebel!
ANDERSON Patriot, sir.
MAJOR Why the hell didn't you name him?

[*He hits* WULLIE. EDDIE *shoves the* MAJOR]

ANDERSON Easy—does none of you wonder why a Patriot Son of
    Liberty would share a meal and memories with tea drinkers and
    traitors?
GEORGE Who be the traitor here?
ANDERSON And who be the King's lap dog?
MAJOR What were the Sons of Liberty but a terrorist gang bent on
    stealin' and tarrin' and featherin'?
ANDERSON I know everyone of you here, you're the ones spoke 'gainst
    the tyranny, but when it came time to stand bold 'gainst tyrant,
    there was no man amongst you!

[GEORGE *spits at* ANDERSON]

DANIEL What do you want?
ANDERSON Justice.
MAJOR You want Wullie?
WULLIE I didn't kill no one!
ANDERSON Then you were one hell of a poor soldier, Wullie.
EDDIE You take Wullie, you take me first.

ANDERSON I may want you first.

DANIEL So what do you want?

ANDERSON I had a brother.

DANIEL We never heard of you so how the hell could we know your brother!

ANDERSON My brother was murdered at Waxhaws, cut to pieces with the rest of them that surrendered.

MAJOR Nobody was murdered at Waxhaws, that was an act of war and men fell in battle.

ANDERSON The slaughter of surrendered men is murder.

GEORGE Do you know some court of law where some soldier's been charged with that by his peers?

MAJOR And convicted?

ANDERSON [laughs] You Loyalists got a habit of confusin' legality and justice.

EDDIE What about King's Mountain?

ANDERSON What about it?

EDDIE Rebels killed Loyalists there. We called quarter and surrendered and they killed us, we threw down our guns and they killed us, we sat down on the ground—

WULLIE And we sat on our hands—

EDDIE And they killed us.

GEORGE You don't call that some kind of justice?

ANDERSON I call it murder on murder, like the boots of a corpse makin' its rounds.

MAJOR So you had a brother, so he died at Waxhaws.

ANDERSON Do none of you understand? The sentence for murder is death. I intend executin' the one of you here, or any one of you here, before I leave tonight.

DANIEL Are you crazy?

ANDERSON What do you think?

[DANIEL *slowly approaches* ANDERSON *as he speaks*]

DANIEL I think you're crazier than hell! You weren't at the Waxhaws, you don't know what the hell happened there! I told you, the Rebels sent a fella out with a little white hankie tied to the tip of a sword. Who the hell could see that? And right then, at the same time, Tarleton's horse went down, ain't that right? And Tarleton under it! We all thought he was dead and we—you're a fightin' man, you must know—it ... it was like a slaughter pen, and a sabre goes through flesh like a hot knife through butter and no one gave the order to stop and ... and ... ain't none of us proud of what happened that day—

[DANIEL *goes to grab* ANDERSON. ANDERSON *kicks out at him, getting him in the mouth, knocking him down*]

ANDERSON But when it was over, well over, some of you went from one pile of bodies to another, pullin' off the dead and killin' the wounded and livin'. And one of the livin' was a fourteen-year-old boy who had time to cry "quarter" 'fore the sabre came down, Do you remember that boy? ... None of you remembers that boy?

DANIEL We don't want to remember. We spend time forgettin'.

ANDERSON Well I can't forget, nor do I want to.

EDDIE Or forgive?

MAJOR There's nothin' to forgive.

GEORGE What about justice for them that was stoned and hanged and died of a tarrin' for remainin' Loyal!

ANDERSON And look what you got for it. Eddie can't even register land.

MAJOR So in the name of justice you come to commit murder on one of us here—well, choose your scapegoat and go!

DANIEL Hold on.

MAJOR The province is peopled with soldiers, and once you leave here, you'll not make the border. So choose!

ANDERSON You choose.

DANIEL One of us?

ANDERSON Or let the responsible one step forward. Was it you?

WULLIE Not Eddie.

DANIEL Shut up, Wullie.

DANIEL Why're you so certain it's one of us here?

ANDERSON A witness.

MAJOR Who?

DANIEL It weren't none of us here!

ANDERSON There's always a witness. Could be one who escaped in the woods. One who didn't beg quarter and lived. Could be one of your own who'd try to barter the name for his life. So—step forward—or choose.

MAJOR We—are not going to choose.

ANDERSON I choose then. I choose ... you, ma'am.

[*He is referring to* ANNIE]

GEORGE No!

DANIEL You can't do that!

ANDERSON An innocent, which is fitting and proper. Historically accurate.

[ANDERSON *carefully leans his long gun on a wagon shaft or barrel close at hand*]

GEORGE No.

ANDERSON I thought royalty lovers would appreciate that.

EDDIE Don't talk about royalty, talk about the rightness of now, this action right now.

ANDERSON Responsibility denied for the death of my brother, denied again by refusin' to choose. Who always pays when them that can, don't? The innocent pay. Step forward, ma'am.

DANIEL Annie had nothin' to do with it!

ANDERSON She pays for your refusal to act. You choose this by refusin' to choose.

GEORGE Wait.

DANIEL Kill me 'stead of Annie!

ANDERSON That wouldn't be justice 'less you be the one.

GEORGE What is it you want?

ANDERSON Responsibility acknowledged, and twice you refuse.

EDDIE Even St. Peter got three cracks at denyin'. Ask the question again.

ANDERSON Let the responsible one step forward.

[*No one moves. He shoves* ANNIE, *she falls down. He aims the pistol at her head*]

MAJOR We'll choose.

[DANIEL, GEORGE, *the* MAJOR, WULLIE *and* EDDIE *move away to consult while* JOAN *approaches* ANDERSON *slowly, tentatively.* ANNIE *is still down. The light will gradually dim on* JOAN, ANDERSON *and* ANNIE, *which isolates the men and* EDDIE]

JOAN Lost. I lost my oldest, Richard, my oldest. Can that which is lost be found? Lost, Edward my youngest, and Richard, he was just standin' there at the end of the walk and he raised his hand in a bit of a wave and then he was gone, and the walk?

MAJOR [*low*] Any of you got a pistol?

DANIEL Got a knife.

JOAN The walk? The walk it was empty, and Edward? Edward lay on the bed and he stared at the ceilin' and Em'ly? There was seven minutes between them and I'd sit in the parlour, it was a wonderful room with ... and ... over there, and here ... [*to* ANDERSON] and do you remember that?

ANNIE Hush, Mama.

JOAN [*to* ANDERSON] You can whisper.

MAJOR You're good with a knife, eh Wullie, at throwin' a knife?

EDDIE There's no way of takin' him 'less he fires at least the pistol.

DANIEL And the person who'd take that ball is Annie. You said we'd choose and I say we do that.

GEORGE Is he right? 'Bout one of you at the Waxhaws?

JOAN Annie would sit in the rocker with both of them, arm round each of 'em, Edward and Em'ly, and Richard would rock 'em, stand behind them and push and the rocker would rock and Richard would sing sweet and clear, clear and sweet
[*sings*] *Hi says the little leather winged bat*
I will tell you the reason that

[*The sound of a child's voice is heard singing faintly, joining* JOAN*'s*]

The reason that I cry in the night
Is because I lost my heart's delight

[*The child's voice continues to sing alone as others speak*]

Hi says the little mourning dove
I'll tell you how to win her love
ANNIE It's alright, Mama, shush.
JOAN [*whispers to* ANDERSON] Do you know that song?

[*The light is now fully on the men and* EDDIE]

GEORGE I mean, if one of you at the Waxhaws did that, I mean, don't that bear on the matter if one of you—
MAJOR No.
GEORGE No?
MAJOR That's his path, not ours.
GEORGE But if the guilty one's here, why—
DANIEL If that person don't choose to step forward then that person don't step forward. Ain't nobody going to point their finger at nobody.
MAJOR We all be guilty and we all be innocent. We were followin' orders and responsibility and murder don't come into it.
DANIEL You was givin' quite a few of those orders back then.
MAJOR They came to me, I passed them on to you.
DANIEL I don't suppose we can choose Tarleton if he ain't here.
MAJOR Tarleton was followin' orders, it's a war, for Christ's sake!
EDDIE Nothin' goes up the ladder, it always comes down.
GEORGE But surely if one of you—
MAJOR I said no!
EDDIE I'll step forward.
GEORGE But you're not the one, Eddie, are you?
DANIEL Get some straws and we'll draw on it.
MAJOR Goddamn it, you don't order a man to his death on the length of a straw, is that civilized?
GEORGE I wasn't there.
DANIEL He wasn't there.

EDDIE So this civilized process of "all is innocent and all is guilty" only applies to them that was actually there?

MAJOR Well, I dunno, I—

EDDIE Eh?

MAJOR I'm thinkin'! Right! Citizen and soldier, all both innocent and guilty in war.

EDDIE And Annie?

MAJOR Not women!

DANIEL Women don't come into it!

MAJOR But the rest of us, we all share in the Waxhaws.

EDDIE Equally?

MAJOR Keep your mouth shut, Eddie, and listen! If we don't do this properly we're no better than the Rebels. The group chooses, agreed?

DANIEL Agreed.

GEORGE Agreed.

MAJOR Agreed. We choose one and that one sacrifices all for the others and Annie. And that one'll die knowin' the Rebel will hang for it. If we have to drag him tied to a horse out of Delaware, we'll do it.

DANIEL Agreed.

GEORGE Agreed.

WULLIE What if I be chose?

DANIEL What if he be chose? Ain't never been a white man hanged for killin' a black.

WULLIE If I get chose, I'll sorely miss seein' that hangin'. I'll wager that'll be a hangin' you'll all miss seein'. Ain't nobody going to see that event.

DANIEL Wullie's right.

MAJOR If Wullie be chose, we take the Rebel's money and assets worth Wullie's thirty-nine years of indentured service to Frank, and give it to Frank's heirs, fair and legal, ain't that the law?

DANIEL It's the law alright.

MAJOR That's right. So—any of us could be chose 'cause we all share in the Waxhaws.

DANIEL Yeah?

MAJOR But—[*he considers* WULLIE] We don't all share in the killin' of

Frank. That was no act of war, that was murder, pure and simple!

[*Light change. The focus is now on* ANNIE, ANDERSON *and* JOAN, *who hums softly as she rocks back and forth*]

ANNIE [*getting up*] Could you kill me lookin' me right in the face?

ANDERSON If I had to.

JOAN Do you believe a lion can lie down with a lamb?

ANDERSON I can see the two of them lyin' down alright, but I can only see the one of them gettin' up.

JOAN [*laughs*] No no no. No no.

ANNIE My brother believed a lion could lie down with a lamb, and both of 'em get up again.

ANDERSON Eddie?

JOAN Not Eddie, no.

ANNIE Richard, the oldest. It was impossible for Richard to sit down at table with Father without havin' words, ugly words, and yet Richard believed lions could lie down with lambs and he saw no contradiction in that. He fought with Arnold at Quebec; he died at Saratoga, least that's what we heard.

ANDERSON A patriot?

ANNIE I saw him once in the prison ship. You don't believe me? I did. I made my way there. I offered somethin'. Them in charge wanted it. I gave it to them. It meant nothin' to me. You could have it too if you want … Afterwards, they let me see him, and after that, I gave it to them again, or they took it. When I saw him, my brother, he told me the worst fightin' he'd seen up 'til then was 'tween two prisoners over a rat. He looked so thin. He laughed.

ANDERSON Why tell me?

ANNIE After he was exchanged he fought under Arnold at Saratoga. We heard that's where he died.

ANDERSON Do you think you can bargain with that?

ANNIE He looked so thin.

[*Lights begin to change to focus on the* MAJOR *and the men*]

ANDERSON [*steps away from the women*] You can't bargain with that.

JOAN Bargain with that!

ANDERSON You have 'til dawn!

MAJOR Alright!

DANIEL I thought the Rebel killed Frank.

GEORGE I thought you thought Wullie did.

DANIEL That was before the Rebel said Frank was his witness.

GEORGE Did he say that?

MAJOR He was playin' with us, gettin' us goin'.

DANIEL Well he was going to kill me if I hadn't the gun right there on the saddle.

MAJOR The Rebel wants the responsible one—or an innocent one— or the one that we choose—so why would the Rebel kill Frank?

DANIEL He'd do it to get on to us!

MAJOR But Wullie here—

WULLIE Didn't do nothin' to Frank!

MAJOR You shot him to get out of indentured service.

WULLIE Then why'd I come to see Eddie?

MAJOR To tell him Frank knew 'bout the certificate Eddie forged sayin' you be a freed runaway Rebel slave.

EDDIE The certificate's good.

WULLIE I come to get Eddie to read my indenture paper. Frank tells me one year service, but I don't trust him. I make my mark thinkin' one year!

MAJOR Who says?

WULLIE I do!

MAJOR Unsubstantiated. You got a white man's word for that?

WULLIE I had to take a white man's word 'cause I can't read!

MAJOR You must have some old darkie round can read, tell you thirty-nine years 'stead of one.

WULLIE I come to Eddie to read it!

DANIEL If Wullie don't know it's thirty-nine years, why'd he kill Frank?

MAJOR Wullie knew!

DANIEL He says—

MAJOR Frank told Wullie thirty-nine years when he signed!

WULLIE No.

MAJOR Told him 'fore he signed.

DANIEL Wullie says no.

MAJOR Unsubstantiated! So if Wullie be guilty of the murder of Frank, and we so find him, I say let Wullie be the one we choose for the Rebel!

EDDIE I could have killed Frank. I was out all day and Frank was a man I wouldn't mind killin'.

GEORGE Keep your mouth shut.

MAJOR We'll vote on it.

EDDIE Who votes?

MAJOR All of us here.

EDDIE Includin' Wullie?

MAJOR The accused don't vote.

EDDIE What're you? Judge? Prosecutor? I don't think you can vote. Not if we want it done proper.

MAJOR Well—

EDDIE I can't vote. I'm confessin' to the murder of Frank Taylor.

MAJOR You can't do that!

EDDIE That leaves Daniel—and you, father.

DANIEL The Rebel killed Frank! You wasn't with me when I seen him under the trees. The hair came up on the back of my neck, was like seein' a ghost, and then he give his horse a bit of a nudge, and when he got clear of the trees, he was just another man like myself. A soldierin' man. I could tell. One of us. That's what I thought.

MAJOR You brought a viper into the nest, Corporal.

DANIEL Well it's a bit late for that now. All I know is here's Eddie sayin' he killed Frank, and you sayin' Wullie killed Frank, and me thinkin' the Rebel killed Frank, and one of us is going to get killed and none of this is gettin' us any further ahead!

MAJOR You don't choose a man for death without some kind of due process and I'm doin' my best to find one!

EDDIE Perhaps there's no such thing.

MAJOR You got no respect for position or placement! There's the reason we lost the war!

DANIEL If we can't volunteer and we're not drawin' straws, nor press-gangin' Wullie, what the hell are we doin'?

GEORGE Would it be right to say ... that some ... not just us here now, but at large, some are more valuable to the community and all ... do you understand what I'm sayin'?

WULLIE This one understands—it's the kind of thing a coloured man don't have no trouble at all understandin'.

GEORGE Such things are generally understood. You can't have people without you have some kind of relationship between people, some kind of rankin', some kind of value put on their contribution and placement.

MAJOR Go on.

GEORGE Does it make some kind of sense that the least valuable to the community be the one that we choose, if choose we must?

MAJOR All to be done equal and democratic.

DANIEL How can that be done with Wullie here?

EDDIE [*low*] Gimme that knife, Daniel.

DANIEL What for?

[DANIEL *slips the knife to* EDDIE]

MAJOR We each of us, Wullie too, makes our case and we assess all of the cases and we vote, each gettin' a vote, agreed?

EDDIE I want you to know that if I get any sense at all, the littlest feeling that things ain't runnin' democratic and equal.

[DANIEL *stands so as to obscure* ANDERSON's *vision as* EDDIE *grabs the* MAJOR *and places the knife momentarily against his throat*]

I'm going to cut your throat. I'm going to kill you dead as I killed Frank.

DANIEL You never did, Eddie.

EDDIE Either I did, or the Rebel did, take your pick.

MAJOR Equal and democratic, I swear it, we each state our case and we vote on it.

[EDDIE *releases the* MAYOR. *Morning light grows on* ANDERSON, ANNIE, *and* JOAN]

JOAN My mother ... my mother spoke of a soft rain, she'd visit the grave of my father with a soft rain fallin'.
No soft rain here. Peltin' rain. Peltin' him who fell. If he fell. [to ANDERSON] I don't know where you lie, Richard. Some field, they buried you in some field some ... For the other one, there's a cross but not close to here, no, and the name is her name on the cross which I don't think I can find, can never go back, far away, another country. [referring to EDDIE] Him, her, I don't know, transformation ... Not my child anymore, not her anymore. [to ANDERSON] Can you help me?

ANDERSON [seizing ANNIE roughly] Choose one or it's Annie!

JOAN Her, yes, that one. She lay on her back and she spread her legs so she could see you. She said you were thin. She said I wouldn't know you. I'd know you. I begged him, [referring to GEORGE] I begged, but he wouldn't, so she did. [referring to herself] Her, her, she listens and looks but the real colour and sound of this place escapes her and there is nothin' inside, everything's ... grey ... goin' grey; glowin' grey, the sky is glowin' now!

ANNIE I guessed you know, but I didn't give you away. You reminded me of a charmin' man I once knew, but he's gone now. They hanged him. I know that. Still ... I'm wonderin' why I didn't give you away. My brother is one of the reasons. And somethin' about you another. And I suppose I was interested in seein' what you were here for, whoever you were. I was curious, like a cat. And you could talk to me and laugh and call me Annie and kill me?

ANDERSON If I had to.

ANNIE Chose to. It's not them choosin', is it? It's you. Will killin' me ease the ache in your heart for your brother? Why not kill us all? Maybe that would wipe away his final terror and pain.

JOAN You were never at Cherry Valley, were you? What's your name? Real name. Name yourself. Are you Richard or Edward? Are you someone I know?

ANNIE Who could I kill to clear Mama's head?

JOAN Oh don't talk of killin', talk of talk and namin' and talk.

ANNIE Why don't you choose to ride out of here?

ANDERSON I'm not finished yet.

JOAN Talk!

[*The light is on the men*]

DANIEL I don't know what to say. Value to the community. I ain't
done much. But I'm young, there's a lot still to come.

MAJOR I can't plead youth, but I'm not old.

GEORGE Age is to come into it then?

MAJOR You see here a man rich and ripe with knowledge and experience, and sharin' it all with them where I live.

GEORGE I'd qualify there if we were talkin' 'bout Boston.

DANIEL But were not.

MAJOR I got the governor's ear and I'm in with the Fifty-five, and in
here [*pointing to his head*] I carry details of land claims that
haven't been writ, and a host of figures and sums and dealin's and
doin's—and if that knowledge be lost, well—or if the power you
hold through me were to go to another not so well disposed
towards the Loyalist interests—

GEORGE I've fought for that interest.

MAJOR But not on the field.

GEORGE No. Eddie though, Eddie has. And I—I provide for the wife
and daughter.

DANIEL Family.

GEORGE I'm of value to them.

DANIEL I'm by myself there too, but when I get buildin' I was
hopin'—What about neighbours? Value to neighbours! Them on
the south, I helped clear stump—

MAJOR I've no wife to be widowed or children orphaned, but there's a
reason for that. I give my all to the state. And you gotta remember that, like the body, a state can lose fingers and toes, an arm
and a leg, but if you strike at the head, the true leaders, then that
state will sicken and die.

DANIEL And they helped me, the neighbours on the south there that
I helped.

JOAN Look at the sky! It's startin' to turn a golden rose. At home a
body'd be hearin' birds by now. Listen. Listen.

ANNIE Listen to me and I'll tell you something. Will you listen?

WULLIE I fetched thirty pound when I be sold on the block at Charleston. I be that valuable! I be so powerful you beat me and you give me the lash and you hang me for things no white man got to answer for. You be so afraid of my words, my words be taken from me and my word don't count in any case or court. I be so valuable even ole Frank Taylor cheat and lie to get my labour. How much do you think you're worth on the block, Major Williams?

GEORGE Eddie? You haven't said nothin' ... Speak up.

EDDIE If I die, you lose my Legion half-pay pension.

GEORGE Eddie ...

EDDIE What is it?

GEORGE You mean more than that.

EDDIE I went to war for you.

GEORGE You know how that came about.

EDDIE And here I am.

GEORGE It was the only way.

EDDIE That's what you said.

GEORGE It wasn't just for me, it was for Annie and your mother.

EDDIE What about Em'ly?

GEORGE You wanted to go! You offered to go! How else were we to survive with the English down our throats 'cause of Richard, and the Rebels at our heels 'cause of me? Was you said you'd go, you said it!

EDDIE I did.

GEORGE So don't just say the half-pay pension.

EDDIE Well, I was willin' to die for you then.

GEORGE Eddie.

EDDIE I'm not willin' to live for you now.

GEORGE Choose me! I'm an old man! I can't pull my weight! I left my life in Boston and I turned my back ... on my oldest son ... I turned my back on Richard ... and Edward, I ... Choose me.

[*Dawn light continues to grow*]

JOAN I hear you, Papa.

ANNIE Major Anderson—Is that your real name? That was the name of John Andre, that most charmin' man I was tellin' you about who was hanged? ... I try to stop doin' that, just to tell things straight, but. You get into the habit of butterin' up and playin' those little games with a man 'cause you never know when you'll need one. Any one. And sometimes I think that I need one. And there John Andre was, under our roof ... and there I was, butterin' him up—We agree that I can be charmin'? Agreed?

JOAN [*to* ANDERSON] Agreed?

ANNIE Why do you think Major Andre took the right road held by the Rebels instead of the left road held by the English?

ANDERSON I think I know why.

ANNIE How would you know? Arnold's man told him left, I heard him.

ANDERSON So why did he?

ANNIE Someone told him different. Somebody convinced him. "Right road's less risky." "Take the right, Major." "My brother, Major, is fightin' with Tarleton in the south, you can trust me, Major." "Take the right, Major." Do you think a person should be held responsible for the hangin' of a man, a man she found charmin', 'cause she just kept sayin' "right" 'stead of "left"? A person could bump into an English regular easy as a Rebel on either road. He was a sweet man. I was lyin' about the trifle. A sweet man. Nevertheless they hanged him.

JOAN Look at the light! It'll flow round us and past us and through us! Look at your hands! [*holding up her hands*] I can see right through the skin! I can see the bones!

[*The rose-coloured light of dawn bathes the stage*]

ANNIE Major Andre was frightened. He knew both roads were risky. When I said right 'stead of left, I ... I was thinkin' of Arnold, not the Arnold who betrayed the Rebel cause, but the Arnold who betrayed my brother Richard. Can you understand that?

MAJOR Vote!

[ANNIE *takes a paper from her pocket*]

ANNIE Look at this. I keep it close. I look at it sometimes. He made a copy, you see, of the plans. In case he was taken. He gave it to me. He trusted me. I was to wait an hour or two after he left, and then make my way to the English. I … didn't do that. Look. It's the West Point plans of defense. I could've got them to the English—but I didn't. I sat in my upstairs bedroom. I looked out of the window. I just held them tight in my hand. I sat there 'til supper.

ANDERSON They wouldn't have made any difference to the war.

ANNIE Maybe they would. Maybe they wouldn't. I know it changes nothin' for Richard. Or Edward. Sweet Major Andre. I wonder if he thought of me at the end … Sometimes I feel his name fillin' my head and pressin' hard on my lips to be spoke … There's nothin' I can do for him now. There's nothin' I can do to put paid to my brothers or you to put paid to yours. We oughta be lookin' to a better world for our children. That's the only way to serve our brothers.

JOAN [to ANDERSON] I can see you now.

ANNIE Go.

JOAN [to ANDERSON] You can go now.

[JOAN holds out her hands. A pause. ANDERSON places the pistol in her hands. He exits]

DANIEL Hey!

MAJOR Jump to it!

[ANNIE picks up the long gun and fires a shot. JOAN passes her the pistol]

ANNIE Tell them how good I am at killin' squirrels, Eddie.

EDDIE She's good.

MAJOR What do you think you're doin'?

ANNIE Not a word, Major. Take all the guns, Mama. Take them down to the water. Throw them in where it's deep. And scatter the horses.

[JOAN leaves with all the guns but ANNIE's]

MAJOR Have you lost your mind?

ANNIE I don't think so.

[EDDIE, WULLIE *and* DANIEL *are passing the rum amongst them*]

DANIEL We're saved, Major, don't you realize that? Jesus, I was gettin' to the point of sayin' ain't none of us worth nothin'— 'cept Wullie here who's worth thirty pounds, eh Wullie?

MAJOR Tell her to put the gun down! We gotta get out and after him, guns or no guns!

EDDIE What for?

MAJOR To capture the bugger!

ANNIE What's he done?

MAJOR Illegal detainment, kidnappin', attempted murder—

[GEORGE *is slowly removing the Rebel's waistcoat. He folds it carefully. He continues to hold it clasped to his chest*]

EDDIE Seemed kind of a Tarleton caper for merry-makin' by an unknown soldier to me—eh Daniel?

DANIEL Me? ... I?

[*He looks at* ANNIE]

ANNIE If ever a man knew merry-makin' it's you.

DANIEL I guess 'twas—but I'm not too happy 'bout losin' the gun, Annie. I only got but the one gun.

WULLIE I want you to know I'd back your charges, Major, but my word ain't worth nothin' in court.

MAJOR George? ... Are you all forgettin' poor Frank? The Rebel killed Frank!

DANIEL You come round to my way of thinkin', have you?

GEORGE If there's evidence we can swear out a warrant.

MAJOR We can't do nothin' standin' here! She's usin' a weapon to detain, to restrict my comin' and goin'—

[JOAN *returns without the guns;* ANNIE *lowers her gun*]

JOAN I saw him. He rode down the path to the road with the whole string of horses behind him. He rode right into the sun. I stood there, watchin' him go, and I saw him. Him and the horses. I put my hand up so, shieldin' my eyes in order to see. He rode on a path of light right into the sun with all of the horses behind him. And a black veil came over my eyes. When it lifted there was only the empty road. He was gone.

MAJOR [*starting to exit*] You think my horses won't come for a whistle? There's sedition here.

EDDIE Is dissent sedition?

MAJOR [*stops and turns to face them*] Let me tell you something. The election slate for the Fifty-five will win, and them that's in the right camp will prosper. You've had your chance. You're makin' a choice right now. This country's going to flower and bloom like a rose in the wreath of Empire, it'll be built on patronage and preferment for that way's as natural as the flower turnin' its face to the sun. And if you don't find that to your likin', my advice to you is remove yourself!

EDDIE Or remove you.

[MAJOR *leaves giving a sharp whistle for his horse; the whistles continue, echoing, getting fainter and fainter*]

DANIEL You're a beautiful girl, will you marry me, Annie?

ANNIE [*laughs*] Never.

[ANNIE *and* DANIEL *move towards the periphery of the space*]

JOAN [*examining her fingers*] Him Her Him Her Her Him.

GEORGE [*still holding the waistcoat to his chest*] I do love you. You know that, don't you? I love you.

[WULLIE *and* EDDIE *begin to take down the trophies of war*]

WULLIE Yorktown fell on October 19th.

EDDIE I guess so.

WULLIE I know so.

EDDIE Waxhaws was my first real engagement.

WULLIE I could see that. You was just a puppy at Waxhaws.

EDDIE Little skirmishes 'fore that.

WULLIE Not the same.

[WULLIE *and* EDDIE *continue to clear the space, not having to leave the stage to do so; they are taking down all the war totems and souvenirs. They are returning the stage to some semblance of its virgin state at the beginning of the play*]

EDDIE You and me, what a couple of asses, volunteerin' for King's Mountain to get away from the Legion, eh Wullie?

WULLIE [*laughs*] That's what we were thinkin'.

EDDIE And after King's Mountain, you carried me through the swamp and the woods back to the Legion.

WULLIE You wasn't that heavy—for a man.

EDDIE You saved my life.

WULLIE We all be takin' turns back then.

JOAN What happened to Em'ly?

EDDIE She's still here, Mama.

JOAN She's gone.

EDDIE She's changed.

JOAN [*looking into* EDDIE's *face*] Eddie. Let me look at your face from a distance.

EDDIE It's a new world, Mama—you gotta look up close.

JOAN Up close.

[JOAN *touches* EDDIE's *face and turns to look at* GEORGE]

Papa?

[*She moves towards* GEORGE]

EDDIE How 'bout you, [*to* WULLIE] you want to see somethin'?

WULLIE What?

EDDIE Somethin'. [*gets out the bloody paper folded in eighths*] Frank was crowin' to me 'bout the thirty-nine years.

WULLIE He was some fella, he was. I remember him at the Waxhaws. [*looks at the paper*] This be Frank's copy of my indenture paper.

EDDIE That's right.

WULLIE How'd you get it?

EDDIE I took it out of his pocket.

WULLIE When?

[EDDIE *doesn't answer.* WULLIE *tears up the paper*]

JOAN [*to* GEORGE] I can hear you.

EDDIE Sierra Leone, you ever hear of that place?

WULLIE Yeah. Africa. They say the Loyalist coloureds that want to go, the English'll take 'em.

EDDIE Yeah? You goin' to go?

WULLIE Nope.

EDDIE [*laughs*] You're crazy.

WULLIE [*laughs*] Yeah, that's right.

JOAN I feel my feet pressin' flat 'gainst the surface of the soil now. I kneel readin' the contours of the skull and listenin' to the words spoke by the man with the missin' jawbone, and the caps of my knees make a small indentation in the dirt.

WULLIE They say the army be enlistin' again.

EDDIE I heard that.

WULLIE To serve in the West Indies.

EDDIE Ah-huh.

[*As they clear areas of the space, the floor seems to glow with a dark rich swirl of colour as the lights are fading*]

WULLIE Are you goin' to go?

EDDIE Nope.

JOAN And the red woman with the baby on her back steps out from under the glade of trees and she holds out a bowl, she offers a bowl full of earth.

WULLIE I suppose we could always stay about here. Try to make a place.

EDDIE We could do that.

[**WULLIE** *reaches out and clasps* **EDDIE**'s *hand.*]

Eat, she says. Swallow.

JOAN And I do.

[*She slowly raises her hands, fingers spread in front of her face*]

[*Blackout*]

APR - - 2010